GW00647720

BEACH FISHING

BEACH FISHING

John Holden

THE CROWOOD PRESS

First published in 1986 by
THE CROWOOD PRESS
Ramsbury, Marlborough
Wiltshire SN8 2HE

© Ocean Publishing 1986

All rights reserved. No part of this publication may be
reproduced or transmitted in any form or by any means,
electronic or mechanical, including photocopying,
recording, or any information storage and retrieval system
without permission in writing from the publishers.

British Library Cataloguing in Publication Data

Holden, John, 1947 –
  Beach fishing.
  1. Saltwater fishing
  I. Title
  799.1′6   SH457

ISBN 1–85223–005–3

Typeset by Inforum Ltd, Portsmouth
Printed in Great Britain

Contents

Introduction

Beaches, estuaries and rocks are the last stronghold of real fishing. These fringes of the sea offer dazzling opportunities for the fisherman who accepts the challenge of seasons and tides. No sport for the faint hearted or those who demand guaranteed catches, beach fishing is ruled by natural forces, not man's whims. There are no artificial stocking programmes to boost the fish population, but neither are there catch limits, close seasons and restricted hours. Beaches are wild, as are the creatures that live on them and in the lapping waves. A bass, cod or even a whiting hooked from swirling breakers is worth more than the biggest carp or trout that ever swam; or so beach fishermen claim. Of course they are biased, but who can blame them?

There are fishermen, old-timers mostly, who say that the quality of beach fishing has fallen. Perhaps they are right: commercial fishing and pollution have reduced the number of fish that swim within casting range of beaches and piers. In the most important sense they are wrong: the pleasure of casting for cod, whiting, bass, tope, flat-fish and the many other species found in our waters is as great as it ever was. Indeed, many of us enjoy fishing more because of the greater demands on time, patience and skill.

The rapid development of new tackle and techniques has brought a technological revolution and a radical change in tactics. Rods, reels, terminal rigs and casting styles are important in their own right; and indeed there are thousands of dedicated fishermen for whom owning the latest rod or adding an extra twenty-five yards to the cast is just as satisfying as hooking fish. Fishing from estuaries, beaches, piers, harbours, rocks and jetties is a blend of Space Age technology and traditional hunting skills. Balanced against that is the fact that today's fisherman is content to land perhaps three or four fish in a day instead of the heavy catches that were common twenty years ago. Dedicated anglers consider this a small price to pay for the tremendous enjoyment of casting baits into saltwater.

Opportunities

Wading into the surf to cast for bass is the only fishing that appeals to a few anglers. Others prefer to enter competitions rather than to fish purely for pleasure. Some would rather fish from a pier than learn to cast the long distances usually necessary for success on an open beach. Which option should the beginner choose? Most definitely he must resist any urge to specialise. First, it is essential to gain a balanced, overall insight into the world of shore fishing. Later he may discover, as the majority of fishermen do, that a general approach is better anyway. While there are benefits in becoming expert in just one small section of the sport, on the whole it is more rewarding to learn something

7

about everything.

Good fishing depends on seasons, weather and the breeding/migratory patterns of fish as well as on baits, tackle and techniques. There are many weeks in every year when bass are unlikely to feed, or they are nowhere within casting range because the water is too cold. Similarly, it is almost impossible to catch cod and whiting south of the Straits of Dover between May and October unless you go far out to sea where the water remains cold throughout the summer. Even then, catches will be poor because the big shoals have migrated north. The man who fishes from the beach for cod during August is unlikely to catch even one fish. But the same spot will produce excellent sport in December.

These examples are very easy to understand even if you have never fished before. But there are patterns that even experienced fishermen tend to forget which also must be considered, or you may fish for hours or even days without getting a bite. Imagine a surf beach in autumn, calm and hot. Good fishing is available for bass, rays and flat-fish, perhaps even a turbot or a tope. Which species should you fish for today? Bass are a bad choice: unless the water is rough they usually stay well beyond casting range. To hook them, wait until the wind blows onshore and produces a steady surf. The swells wash sand-eels out of the sand; bass move close inshore to attack them. Therefore, by casting sand-eel baits into the white water you can be fairly confident of success. It is a logical process of cause and effect.

Today the water is so calm that you are unlikely to catch anything except a flat-fish. The knowledgeable angler stays at home until after dark, then he will fish the calm water using mackerel, sand-eel, crab or squid baits. He knows that big rays and tope – and yes, perhaps even a big solitary bass – cruise inshore at night to feed on small creatures that emerge from their sandy burrows under cover of darkness. As before, success is based on an understanding of natural history.

Priorities

When and where are just as important as how to fish; often they are a more valuable part of the equation. The priority in learning to become an expert shore fisherman is to think about your sport in terms of wind, weather, seasons and how fish move and feed. There are broad trends and patterns to discover, such as how sea conditions vary from summer to winter, the annual migration of cod, bass and other major species. There is a local aspect as well.

Do you know where sand-eels, worms and crabs live on your favourite beach? How does a south-west wind affect the fishing? Where do the bass feed? Which is the best time and tide for cod and whiting? These and a thousand more questions you must identify and answer for yourself. Explore, look, listen and ask questions. Other fishermen are usually quite willing to assist; there is far less secrecy in shore fishing than you might imagine.

Nothing is difficult to learn, but it does

(Opposite) Cod migrate inshore during cold weather.

take time. Two years is about the minimum period in which a shore fisherman can develop his basic skills, and ever afterwards the sport demands continuous attention to detail. I say this not to deter you from becoming a shore fisherman but rather to point out the reality of the situation: modern beach fishing calls for expertise and dedication.

Practical skills

In contrast to the natural history aspect, tackle making, casting, bait collection and other practical skills are quite easy to learn. Modern rods and reels offer high performance and reliability at moderate expense. Terminal rigs and accessories are available in all good tackle shops and can be made at home if you prefer, as most experienced men do. Perhaps the single most important practical skill to learn is casting. Of course it is not necessary to cast huge distances every time you go fishing, but on balance most beaches produce a lot more fish if you can throw a bait 100 yards at least. If that seems a long, long way at the moment, do not worry. Today's tackle plus a basic but efficient style like the Off-ground or Pendulum technique make it easy for anybody to cast that far at least. Many fishermen cast over 150 yards, and tournament champions have already achieved 275 yards with specialised equipment.

(Opposite) Harbours produce as many fish as the open sea.

1 Rods and reels

Rods

Rod selection is a hazardous proposition for any beginner because the majority are wrong for him personally, which is a different matter from being good or bad in their own right. Some are too long, too stiff, too slow or too fast in action; they either cast too powerfully or lack the strength to throw even eighty yards. Handles are too long or too short to be comfortable.

But you have to start somewhere, and common sense dictates caution at this stage. Do not buy an expensive or specialist rod until you know exactly which length, power and action suits you best. Opt instead for a semi-carbon or fibreglass rod 11½–12 feet long, strong enough to cast 5–6oz and of medium-fast action with a flexible tip and a stiff handle. If the rod is constructed as a long tip and detachable butt, the best handle material is either high tensile aluminium alloy or economy carbon. Well made but unsophisticated, such a rod is the perfect choice for learning how to catch fish from the seashore. Daiwa's Moonraker and Paul Kerry glass fibre models are excellent examples of off-the-peg rods that combine performance with modest price.

Second-hand rods are a welcome alternative for beginners on a tight budget. However, no matter how cheap the rod, no matter how good an investment it seems to be, do make sure that it conforms to the basic design requirements. Be wary of long, super-powerful tournament rods and blanks at this stage. Many are up for sale because their owners cannot cast them; some are unsuitable for fishing anyway, no matter how well you cast.

Before you can assess the various rods and blanks on sale, you must learn to cast reasonably well. But before you start practising you must have a suitable rod, otherwise all your efforts result in nothing but backlashes, frustration and poor distances. It seems an impossible situation. However, there are basic rules on rod selection which are guaranteed to lead even the rawest beginner through the minefield.

Rod length and handle spacing affect the amount of leverage you can exert during a cast. Too long a rod strains your muscles; an unnecessarily short rod wastes power. The same logic applies to the handle: if your hands are set too far apart, they cannot produce a fast enough whip at the end of the casting action. Hands set too close together seriously reduce your casting power.

Ideal rod length for most beach fishermen regardless of their casting skill is between 11½ and 12 feet with a corresponding handle of 27 to 33 inches measured from butt cap to reel. Actually, 29 to 30 inches is the perfect spacing for most beach fishermen who standardise on the popular 5¼oz sinker. However, rough water and onshore winds sometimes demand sinkers up to

Butt stiffness test.

with a stiffish lower half and a flexible tip. Support the middle of the rod with your left hand, rest the butt cap on the ground then push firmly with your right hand half-way along the butt section. A firm push (60–80lb) should flex the butt between one and three inches. Reject a rod that simply folds up with no resistance, or is so stiff that you cannot make an impression on it.

A flexible tip permits easy casting of a wide range of sinkers, cushions mistakes and smooths out the release phase of the cast. Later on you will discover that a responsive tip is essential for pendulum casting. There are no easy tests for tip flexibility, but blank diameter is a reasonably good guide: the best modern blanks measure 3–4mm. Beware of any beach rod with a diameter over 4mm (measured just below the tip ring) – it will be dull and/or rigid.

Choose a rod with two equal length sections joined by a factory fitted, well whipped spigot, or buy a long tip plugged into or spigotted to a short handle. ABU-style lightweight metal ferrules with a locking screw are acceptable, but the majority of cheap ferrules and flimsy Oriental overlapping joints (half of the rod pushes directly into the other) are too weak to withstand hard casting.

With few exceptions, modern beach rods are fitted with good quality rings with ceramic, silicon carbide or hardened steel liners. Typical examples are Fuji aluminium oxide or SiC, Hopkins and Holloway Seymo, and Daiwa Dynaflo. Ring sizes and spacings are computed for multiplier or fixed spool work. Fixed spool casting needs four or five large, well spaced rings between 16mm and 50mm in diameter, the butt ring being no nearer to the reel than

8oz. The more weight you cast the more leverage you need, so it pays to choose a rod with a slightly over-long butt. Shift your left hand up or down the handle to produce exactly the right amount of leverage for the sinker in use.

Good casters seem effortless but they channel quite a bit of muscle power into the rod and through to the sinker. A stiff, powerful rod is difficult to master but produces exceptional distances. A soft, over-flexible rod butt simply sponges up power although it will compensate for mistakes. To get the best of both worlds, choose a rod

40 inches. Seven or eight rings grading from 25 to 30mm at the butt to 12mm on the tip are preferred for multiplier work.

Beach reels

The choice is between multiplier and fixed spool. Backlash has virtually disappeared with the introduction of magnetic and centrifugal brakes, so do not be deterred from buying a multiplier on the basis that it is difficult to control. As long as you buy a casting model not a boat reel, there

Twelve foot, medium-fast rods for fixed spool and multiplier casting.

should be no difficulty in making it cast long distances. Of course there are significant differences between stationary and revolving spools. The fixed spool is less prone to backlash, less sensitive to tuning and quicker on the retrieve. Multipliers are smoother, better balanced and more precise. Some anglers prefer a fixed spool, others a multiplier, many use both. The important questions are which is better for distance work, and which reel is easier to master?

Distance

There is very little to choose between fixed spool and multiplier reels in pure distance terms. Both hold their own on the beach, and even in tournaments they run fairly close. Current records are 250 yards for the fixed spool with the multiplier some 30 yards ahead. In the 125–175 yard band, a realistic target for the beach, there is absolutely no difference in cast length. Given a good casting style, multipliers are docile and backlash-free; no more difficult or demanding than a fixed spool.

The sticking point is not so much whether the fixed spool or the multiplier suits you better. Far more important, is the individual model you choose compatible with long range techniques? Most saltwater fixed spool reels guarantee excellent results, but with multipliers you have to be more careful. Some are incapable of delivering the goods no matter how hard you try. The finest big-game boat fishing multiplier costing hundreds of pounds will not cast as far as the cheapest reel designed for beach work. Such differences ought to be self-evident, but every year beginners make the same old mistakes.

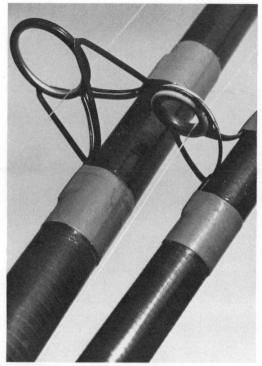

Dynaflo and Fuji lined rings for long range casting.

Multipliers

Most beaches can be safely fished with 250 yards of 12–18lb nylon; a small reel holding that casts much further and more controllably than one that swallows 500 yards of 25lb line. Next comes basic design: there are boat reels, beach reels and some that do both. An all-round reel might well suit you, but make sure you avoid boat multipliers with heavy brass spools, mammoth line capacity and no cast controls. Insist on a reel with a built-in casting controller, either magnetic or centrifugal. Plain old-fashioned reels with lightweight plastic and alloy spools are capable of excellent results, but life is much easier if you can literally dial in some casting control or smooth line flow with interchangeable brake blocks. Braking systems boost confidence, and confidence is a key factor in learning to cast.

Choose a lightweight, one-piece spool running on ballraces or bronze bushes. High-speed gearing makes it easier to retrieve your terminal rig across rough ground. Higher priced reels are a fine investment because they last longer, perform better and are backed by the manufacturer's after sales service.

Multiplier tuning

Tuning is the technique of producing maximum spool speed without creating too much risk of backlash. The more free-running a spool becomes, the less room exists for error. A fast spool generally casts further, therefore one side effect of tuning for safe control is some loss of yardage. Initial casting exercises hardly exceed 140 yards anyway, so by deliberately restricting speed for now you build in a fair amount of insurance. When a slow-running multiplier still backlashes every cast, you can be pretty sure there is a major fault somewhere in your style. Correct that rather than blame the reel.

Open the reel, wipe the ends of the spool spindle and clean out the ballraces. Squirt a little SAE20/50 or SAE90 motor oil into the races, smear a drop on each end of the spindle then reassemble the reel. Adjust the bearing cap until the spindle develops a slight end-float. Now load on your line,

15

High performance beach multiplier – Penn 940 Levelmatic.

starting with a uni-knot to the spool core. Wind on line evenly until the reel is comfortably full. Attach a shock leader. Finally tape down the leader end, flip the reel out of gear and spin the spool by hand. It should run smoothly and not too quickly.

Start by tuning the spool for maximum control. If your reel has magnetic brakes, dial in the highest control number or wind the sideplate adjuster fully clockwise. Centrifugal braking is determined by the size and number of blocks inside the reel. Make your initial adjustment while the reel is stripped down for lubrication. Slide

one large block on to each support bar. As your casting skill develops, gradually back off the magnet dial or change to smaller brake blocks.

Thumb control

Some reels sit low on the rod and others perch high on their frames. You cannot cast properly unless your thumb is wrapped around the spool. Best of all, check spool height before you buy. Otherwise keep line level within comfortable limits.

Everyday beach fishing should not impose any particular strain on your thumb, but now and again a cast goes wrong and line skids away too soon. Powerful rod, big cast and slipping leader are a sure recipe for a burned thumb. Once wounded, most anglers are wary of a reel or even frightened of it. The remedy is easy enough: smooth out your casting style to eliminate spool pressure and if necessary protect your thumb with a piece of rubber tube cut from an old household glove.

Line tension

Even line tension and level spooling are essential for multiplier control. Level-wind reels automatically spread line across the spool but they do not control tension. Whichever kind of reel you use, learn to run the incoming nylon between finger and thumb. Apply steady, modest pressure so that line packs down reasonably tightly. Manual line-lay feels awkward at first but soon becomes second nature. Loose, uneven line guarantees backlash no matter how well you tune a multiplier.

Multiplier spool properly locked down for powerful casting.

Fixed spools

Engineering quality and service back-up are important points to consider. They alone might well justify spending £30–40 on your first reel instead of £15–20 on a cheap and cheerful model that falls apart in six months. Fixed spool gears are always under severe stress due to the mechanical principles of the reel. You cannot expect long, reliable life from cheap metal and ill-cut gear teeth.

Choose a spool of at least 2½in diameter. Small spools strangle a potentially big cast by imposing too much rim friction on flowing line. Experts choose the largest salt-water models and cram them with line. Special tuning techniques ensure maximum line speed and minimum spool rim friction. Such steps are unnecessary while you learn to cast, but bring dividends when your casts exceed 150 yards.

Reduced casting power and cut fingers are a direct result of a spool that skids against its drag plates in mid-cast. Either the reel's drag should lock the spool for powerful casting, or you should modify the reel with an external locking gadget. Bale arms have a nasty habit of snapping shut in mid-cast. To prevent broken lines and lost tackle, fixed spool anglers either cut off the bale arm wire or choose a reel like the Mitchell 498/499 with a manual pick-up roller. Penn now offer a manual bale arm conversion for the Spinfisher 850SS reel.

Setting up

A well set-up fixed spool casts further, throws fewer spider's webs (clumps of

Full spool, locked drag washers and deep finger grip are essential for long casting and easy control.

Magnetic brake adjustment on Penn 970 multiplier.

loose line that catch in the butt ring) and reduces line twist. The golden rule of fixed spool casting is to choose a line as light as you can safely use, bearing in mind the beach, tidal force and size of fish, then cram on as much as the reel can handle without sloughing off loose coils.

Saltwater fixed spool reels swallow such huge amounts of thin nylon that it is essential to back out the bottom of the spool before you wind on 250 to 300 yards of main line. Use old nylon, Dacron or even thin string. Make sure the backing is tight, even and concentric with the spool core.

Finger protection

Line release is second only to poor loading as a cause of lost control. A bare index finger cannot safely withstand a big cast. Even a 100 yard lob with a 5oz sinker builds up enough pressure to raise a blister. Angle of line grip is also important; the leader should form an angle of less than 90 degrees as it lies around your finger. Hold the reel with its stand clamped between your first and second, or second and third fingers. The leader forms an acute angle across your index finger which is fully protected by a leather guard. Make your own guard from a cut-down glove, or buy a finger stall from the chemist.

Line twist

All fixed spool reels twist line, some worse than others. You cannot eliminate twist but you can reduce it to acceptable limits. The best trick is to wind on line under modest tension. Run incoming line between finger and thumb so that it packs down quite hard on the spool. Finger pressure also combs the majority of twists into the last few yards of main line. Cut them off after each fishing session.

2 Essential tackle

Line

Apart from its obvious function of connecting terminal rig to reel, line is enormously important in casting. A minor shift in line diameter adds or takes tens of yards from the cast. By matching line diameter

Fifty pound shock leader attached to fifteen pound main line with streamlined Uni knots.

to the beaches you fish and to your rod and reel, you could gain extra yardage without really trying.

An effortless pendulum cast with 5oz of lead running on 18lb line (about 0.40mm diameter) should produce steady 150 yard casts without baits. With exactly the same rod, reel and casting weight, a much thicker 30lb line would reduce casting range by anything up to 60 yards. Conversely, thin 10lb monofilament would add about 30 yards to the original 150 yard maximum.

Line specification is a compromise between long casting performance and the demands of the sea. Everyone could add 50 yards to his present distances by changing down to 4–6lb line. But how many fish would he lose? How many sets of terminal tackle would be trapped by minor snags on the sea-bed? On the other hand, there is no need for 25–35lb line to haul dabs, whiting or even heavy cod across clean sand, mud and shingle; and you would lose a lot of distance by fishing so heavy. In all, it makes sense to pick a line whose safe breaking strain balances nicely against casting performance; 0.30–0.40mm (12–18lb breaking strain) almost always fits the bill.

Shock leader

Even 18lb line poses a problem in long range casting: as soon as you build any real power into the cast, the line snaps. Counter this by relieving the main line of direct casting stress. Instead of tying thin line directly to sinker or trace, insert a heavy shock leader between the terminal tackle and spool. Make the cast on heavy line then let the sinker fly out on lighter nylon.

Shock leaders add a significant measure of casting safety. Left to its own devices in free flight, a cracked-off sinker carries 300 yards with ease and you can never control its direction. Without a leader, a powerful caster would machine gun the beach or practice field with lethal chunks of lead. *Always use a shock leader with thin running lines.* Attach the leader with the knot shown, which is tough, easy to tie and streamlined for smooth running through the rod rings. For absolute security, insist on at least six full turns of heavy line around the spool when the tackle is set up ready to cast.

Safe breaking strain is reckoned by multiplying sinker weight by ten, and calling the result pounds. Thus, a safe leader for 5oz is 50lb monofilament nylon. Sometimes you do not need to cast really hard, so lighter leaders might be safe on an uncrowded beach. As a rule though, err on the pessimistic side. On the other hand, very few casters need more than 50lb line regardless of how much sinker weight they use.

Line specification

Monofilament, the only line worth using on the beach, comes in a rainbow of colours, brands and quality. Some lines are harsh, others soft. There is no hard and fast rule for selection, but certainly while you learn to cast steer away from expensive brands except for shock leader. No matter how careful you are, a few casts will backlash and ruin a whole spool of line. Cheap

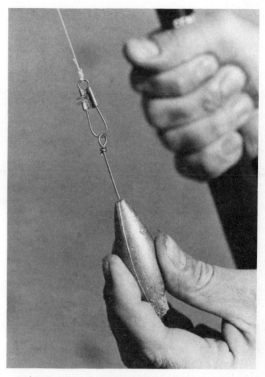

A 5¼oz long tailed bomb for beach fishing and casting practice.

stuff can be replaced for £0.50; 250 yards of premium-grade monofilament costs over £7.00.

Cheap line never combines every feature of a perfect monofilament: even diameter, good strength in relation to diameter, suppleness, abrasion resistance, long life, excellent knotting power and reliability. You get only what you pay for; in cheap brands that means choosing a compromise. As far as learning to cast is concerned, reasonable suppleness, even diameter and knot strength head the list of priorities.

Sinkers

Tournament casters find that just ¼oz makes ten yards difference to their maximum distances. Some choose 5oz, some 5¼oz; others hit peak performance with a full 6oz. There is no need to carry sinker selection to such extremes while you learn to cast or for everyday beach work, but it still pays to choose your practice weight with some care.

A sinker must be light enough to cast without straining your muscles, but heavy enough to make the rod 'work' under moderate casting power. It is easier to time your cast with a reasonably heavy chunk of lead than with a lightweight sinker. In the early days you need all the help you can get, and the right sinker is a tremendous ally.

Five ounce sinkers are ideal for casting practice and general beach work. A rod balanced to cast that much lead gives excellent, easy distance coupled with the bite sensitivity and fighting power to handle big fish while retaining enough action and delicacy to make catching small fish a pleasure. In addition, it has enough backbone in reserve to throw 7–8oz when rough weather and heavy water overwhelm standard sinkers.

Throwing a bait far enough is only half the battle. Making it stay put in fast tides and rough water is another matter. Also, most fish hook themselves against the inertia of the terminal rig. Here too a sinker in the 5–6oz band offers the ideal balance between mechanical efficiency and sport. However, grip wires moulded into the sinker are necessary to counteract tidal pressure and wave force.

If you are new to beach fishing, start fishing with 5–5½oz streamlined bombs: plain for casting practice and slow-water fishing, grip-wired for general fishing. Beachbomb, Aquazoom, Breakaway and Aquapedo are all excellent and should be fitted with swivelling wires rather than fixed spikes for easier retrieve.

Sinker attachment

In allowing a sinker to escape from even a modest cast you turn loose enough energy to smash roof tiles, bury the lead a foot in soft ground or kill someone. It is your personal responsibility to be safe. That

Fine wire Aberdeen-type hooks are perfect for routine beach fishing.

means picking the right place to practise, using a leader and inserting a strong metal link between leader and sinker tail loop. A leader alone does not guarantee safety; its strength and reliability are destroyed by the wrong knot or by subjecting the knot to abrasion.

Field practice hardly abrades a knot. Most of the time you walk up to the lead rather than drag it back through the grass. Beach fishing is another matter because the knot is chafed by sand, grit and rocks every time you reel in. Three or four 100 yard retrieves across rough ground reduce knot strength by 75 per cent. Cast number five snaps and the sinker whirrs out of control down the beach.

Always use a split ring or strong clip between sinker and leader. Check for quality – not all clips are as good as they look. The same goes for link swivels, which are notoriously vulnerable to corrosion and sudden failure. Tie good knots and check them frequently. Palomar and uni-knot are an excellent choice, strong, easy to tie and reliable.

Home-made beach tripod. A bag of stones gives extra stability.

Hooks

Eyed hooks offer the widest selection of bends, wire thicknesses, sizes and steel finishes. As a group, hooks with a direct attachment ring cannot be beaten. Spade ends and whipped hooks do have specific advantages for matchmen and light line anglers but they are nowhere near so versatile, nor are they as easy to use. Ordinary Aberdeens, Vikings, O'Shaughnessy, Kirbys, Baitholders . . . all the world's favourite hooks are made with eyes. Anglers like them that way. Certainly they are easy to tie, quick to change and

best suited to beginners. Preferred knots are the old stalwarts used for tackle assembly in general: uni-knot, tucked half-blood and Palomar.

The eye itself can be a serious disadvantage in worm fishing. Other soft baits suffer as well, but lugworms, harbour rag and silvers are acutely sensitive to the size of that metal ring. Old-style hooks like the O'Shaughnessy, Model Perfect and Baitholder are almost sure to pop even a giant lugworm threaded around the bend, up the full length of the shank and on to the snood. Hooks of this type are impossible to use with small silver ragworm because wire thickness exceeds the diameter of the worm.

Eyed hooks most suitable for beach fishing include Breakaway's Spearpoint, Mustad Viking 79515, Partridge MW and various brands of Aberdeen. It matters little whether an eye lies straight or angled. Wire thickness and ring diameter are what count, and all these hooks are adequate no matter which baits you use. There is little to be gained by resorting to whipped, plain shank hooks for average ragworms and lugworms, sand-eels and crabs. The slight deterioration in bait presentation as compared to a whipping is minimal and more than offset by an eyed hook's greater strength.

Otherwise excellent eyed hooks are often ruined by tying them on to the trace with a bad knot. The thicker the monofilament, the more important it is to tie the smallest, neatest knot you can manage. Sharp ends of nylon and massive coils of line snaking around the eye are more nuisance than the wire diameter itself.

The Palomar is particularly easy to tie, so simple in concept and execution that anglers find it hard to believe the quoted ninety per cent strength. Uni-knots are a little harder to form and tighten, but they too produce a quick, reliable joint in all breaking strains of nylon. Both knots produce a tag end of line that lies parallel to the main snood. The knot barrel is neat enough not to interfere with worms and other soft baits. Another point in the Palomar's favour is that two strands of line form around the hook eye, cushion the knot and help to ward off sea-bed and fish tooth abrasion.

Instead of trimming the knot as tight as possible, leave $\frac{1}{4}$–$\frac{3}{4}$in of line sticking out. Thread worms up the trace then ease them back gently until you feel the sprig of nylon digging into the skin. Now the bait is pretty well immune to sliding back down the shank unless you cast viciously. Lugworm, ragworms and silvers respond well to this treatment. Sand-eels and crabs, even fish strips, also benefit to some extent.

Rod rests

Today's beach rods are light and easy to handle but you still need a solid rod rest. Your sense of touch is far more sensitive than any indicator system, so why not dispense with the rest? Unfortunately, it is a classic case of theory being light years away from everyday practicality. It makes no difference whether your rod and reel weigh 12oz or 12lb. When the sinker is anchored in the sea-bed and water pressure builds up over 80, 100 even 150 yards of line, rod tip leverage becomes enormously powerful. Ten minutes of bracing the rod against a fierce ebb current is enough to beat the toughest of fishermen. Invest in a solid rest or spend time in the garden shed and make your own. Get a robust rod holder now, and save losing your temper later.

(Opposite) A warm, waterproof suit for winter fishing.

The perfect rod rest does not exist. Every year some revolutionary new design comes along then fades as everyone goes back to the old faithfuls. Besides, most 'new' models are based on one of three principles: forked pole, tripod and sandspike. Sandspikes have only one point in their favour: they are easy to carry. The weakness lies in the length of blank left unsupported above the rod's foregrip. Even a light breeze sets the tip vibrating, and anything over Force 4 creates so much bouncing that it is almost impossible to spot small bites. Rod tips sit so high above the beach that you strain your neck watching them.

Some time ago I switched from tripods to long forked rests. Mine is a 6 foot piece of one inch aluminium alloy tube with a simple crosspiece on top to hold two rods securely. Allowing for enough alloy pushed into the sand and shingle for absolute security, the crosspiece supports the rods at a height of about $4\frac{1}{2}$ feet. That is quite a critical figure and should be considered before you buy or make your own rest.

If your rods are at least $11\frac{1}{2}$ feet long, a pole with 4 to 5 feet beach clearance allows an adjustment of rod angle to accommodate almost every wind and weather condition, and permits some fine tuning of bite detection. In reasonably calm weather, set the rod high on the fork so that the maximum length of blank extends beyond the crosspiece. Minute bites show up. Provided the rod butt is pushed a couple of inches into the sand and the rest itself is dug in deep, such an arrangement withstands all but the strongest tidal pressure.

If the tide is too strong and/or the wind is blowing so hard that the tip flaps, move the rod butt cap further away from the rest. The tip sits lower, leaving less of it above the crosspiece. Although bite sensitivity drops marginally there is a dramatic reduction in tip bounce and in the tide's effect. It also helps if the rod lies pointing downwind or in the same direction as the tide run. When the rod is adjusted to lie parallel with the beach and at right angles to the line, security and sensitivity are markedly improved in bad conditions. Anglers routinely offset their rods rather than point the tip straight out from the beach. Even in calm conditions a few degrees offset fine-tunes your system.

No rod rest helps improve bite detection unless you stand in the right place. The trick is not to look out to sea but to sight along the beach instead. Then you can pick up every twitch on the tip. This is specially important at night and in strong winds when bite detection is difficult enough anyway. Another trick besides the obvious one of painting the tip white or a fluorescent colour for extra visibility, is to fish two rods side by side on the same rest so that the tips lie within six inches of each other. By comparing the movement of one tip with the other you can often see bites that otherwise would escape notice.

The long forked pole holds its own on any beach that is soft enough, but a tripod wins every time on hard ground and concrete. Tripods are plagued by design weaknesses, usually affecting the joints and hinges. Go for quality even if it means carrying a little more weight. And, as with forked rests, make sure the rod holder is tall enough. The best tripod on general sale is the Breakaway. Its swivelling head allows full control of rod angle in every direction.

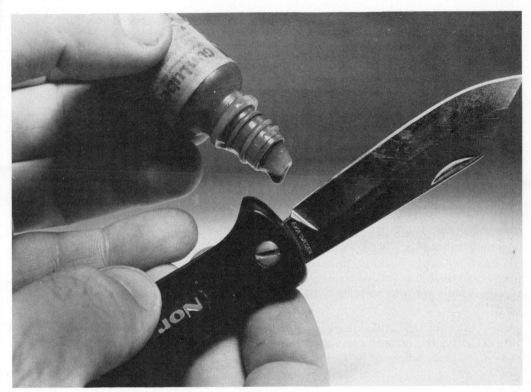

Normark stainless steel folding knife. The hinge requires regular oiling.

Essential accessories

Beach fishing tackle can be as simple or as complex as you care to choose. Advanced design rods, highly tuned reels, bass rods, specialist float and spinning tackle are yours for the asking. Basically though, very little is essential apart from the standard rod, reel, line and terminal tackle already described. But there are a few accessories and gadgets that make life more comfortable on the beach and certainly do help you catch more fish.

Successful fishing is often a matter of playing a waiting game. Sometimes beach fishermen stay out for days at a stretch, and 12 to 18 hour sessions are about average for cod and winter species in general. A big umbrella is highly desirable not only to shelter you and your tackle from the rain but even more importantly to ward off wind and cold. It is the wind chill factor that threatens a beach fisherman's comfort, not necessarily low temperature itself. Buy the biggest, strongest umbrella you can find, preferably one fitted with a nylon skirt that stops wind creeping inside.

On balance, beaches fish better at night so a powerful lamp is essential. Paraffin pressure lamps are standard issue among anglers, the most popular models being Optimus, Tilley and Hipolito. Their 350–500 candlepower output provides more than enough light for baiting, casting and landing fish. Heat output is also substantial – a major bonus for winter fishing.

To complete your creature comforts, buy a good pair of knee length rubber boots or waders. Fitted with insulated inserts, they keep your feet warm and dry and are much healthier than heavily insulated moon boots which, warm as they are, tend to make feet swell if worn for too long. A one-piece waterproof nylon suit or two-piece outfit of the same material wards off wind and rain without being so stiff and

bulky that casting becomes impossible. Underneath in cold weather go fleecy insulated jacket and trousers such as Helly Hansen Polar Wear. And don't forget the hat: sixty per cent of body heat escapes through the top of your head.

Tools of the trade include a sharp filletting knife, pliers with sidecutters and a pair of long handled forceps for unhooking, oilstone for hook sharpening, a kit of reel and lamp spares, screwdriver and reel oil. These along with spare tackle should be stored in plastic boxes with watertight lids. Spares, tackle in general, food, drink and bait are stored and carried in either a rigid tackle box that doubles as a seat or better still in a tough rucksack which is much easier to carry long distances.

3 Casting

Nobody fishes for long without realising that casting is one of the most important skills of the beach game. Of course there are times when fish feed within spitting distance. Unfortunately, many anglers think that they always behave this way and as a result they cannot be persuaded to learn a style more advanced than the traditional overhead thump. Good casters have the option of casting short, medium or to extreme range as conditions dictate. They can choose exactly where to drop the bait: behind the backwash, in a gully at 90 yards or on the far slope of a sandbank at extreme range. The sheer versatility of long distance casting more than justifies the effort of learning modern techniques.

The essence of casting

A rod is a mixture of lever and spring, characteristics that operate together but always with a see-saw effect. When a rod works at peak performance in its spring mode, it is a poor lever; and when it is a solid, powerful lever, a blank shows hardly any springiness. The art of good casting lies in balancing the two so that they work for rather than against you.

Until a blank is flexed to the point where its fibres lock, power input is wasted. Hit into the cast earlier and most of your effort is wasted because the springy side of the blank's character mops it up and wastes it. All good casters learn to feel for that locking sensation before they turn on the power. A good casting style should be a one – two action of bending the blank then adding the main power stroke. Get it even half right and you cannot fail to throw a respectable distance. Bend, lock and accelerate an ordinary glass fibre beach rod even moderately well and it will automatically cast at least 120 yards.

Long range casting is simply the means of making a rod work along those lines. No secrets are involved; there are no complicated scientific formulae to learn. Make the rod bend *before* you dial in the main power, and the sinker has no option but to fly a long, long way. If you approach it from that angle, the arms-and-legs aspect of technique are so much easier to understand and put into practice.

I do not recommend any particular casting style to you. You must decide which best suits your physique and where you fish. Besides, there is no such thing as *the* pendulum cast, *the* South African and so on. You develop your personal variation along those themes. However, you cannot do so until you learn the mechanics involved in making the rod work. Concentrate on this very easy exercise, and do not write it off as too silly and obvious to bother about. It is the foundation of every powerful casting style including the most advanced of tournament techniques. Even in its simplest form it whips a 5oz beach rig well over 150 yards.

Step I – wrong. *This traditional way of holding the rod is inefficient.*

Step I – right. *Altering the layout of rod and arms doubles the rod's arc and makes the body work properly.*

Step 1

For comparison, here is the starting position for a traditional cast. Power comes from the left hand pulling and the right punching. Nothing wrong with that except that the rod is straight and springy rather than bent and locked. The next step is to arrange for the rod to be under load at this push/pull position.

Step 2

Reach back as far as you can and lower the rod tip. Prevent slack line by tossing the sinker away from the tip at the same time, so that it lies in a straight line with the blank on a three to four foot drop. Check that your left elbow is high and the right arm is straight but not strained.

Step 3

Without looking at the rod, pull the han-

The full layout of tackle for off-ground casting.

dle forward with your right hand as if you were throwing a spear. Your left hand will extend away from your shoulder, and the right arm will bend ready to punch. During this pull forward you will feel the rod begin to lock. Concentrate on that sensation. When your arms are back to their original overhead thumping position, the rod seems to be alive and eager. This is because the blank's fibres are locked.

Step 4

Punch and pull, release the line and follow through. The tackle flies much further than before, without effort and much more smoothly because the rod worked properly. Practise, progressively extend the power arc by swivelling around further before you drop the sinker on the ground and finally, once that sensation of bending and locking is second nature, read about whichever specialist technique you want to try.

Body power

Good casters are totally relaxed. Certainly they flick the rod in a powerful arc that drives the tackle skyward, but they do not strain themselves nor do their reels backlash every cast. Their secret – and probably it is *the* secret of good casting – is that they use their bodies rather than their arms alone.

Body weight alone can add 30 to 40 yards to a cast. Go back to the Step 2, but this time on the layout make a conscious effort to extend your body and tackle away from the sea. Feel your weight come on to the right leg. Your left heel rises and the right knee bends a little.

Pull through and cast exactly as before, and concentrate on transferring body weight from right leg to left. Feel yourself literally adding weight to the casting action. The rod whips through faster even though your arms work no harder. Be particularly careful about head action and left elbow height. Without a definite aiming point and a full power stroke from the left hand you cannot achieve full rod efficiency, smoothness or power.

Consider the action of the left hand. Most important, it greatly improves the efficiency of the rod blank by forcing it to operate over the longest possible arc, which automatically boosts power and makes timing far less critical. By pulling the rod forward in spear throwing fashion to full left arm stretch you delay that final whiplike arm action which flicks the blank over and rockets the sinker away.

All good casts drive the sinker high into the air. Head angle and the aerial aiming mark contribute greatly towards that, and the left hand should then naturally make its own contribution. If you get your head around early in the cast and look up, the left hand works better.

Body rotation

Instead of laying out the cast as before, force your upper body round further so that your shoulders lie parallel with the water's edge. Bend your right knee and dip at the waist. Almost force your body into a semi-crouch so that you feel coiled up like a strong spring ready to unwind itself behind the cast. Toss the sinker away into its new position as shown in the picture. The precise angle does not matter too much; similarly, the exact degree of body rotation also depends on physique and personal preference.

Off-ground cast

Layout.

Pull through, spear throwing fashion.

Punch and pull.

Release and follow through.

Body rotation adds more power.

tip points to that imaginary aiming mark in the sky and the sinker flies high and straight. If you finish the cast in roughly this position every time, there is a 90 per cent chance that your style is developing nicely. With practice, distances should creep into the 130s within a few weeks. Given more practice and a longer rod, this style which is known as the South African cast is easily capable of breaking the 200 yard mark and is surprisingly good for all-round fishing even though the sinker and baits are laid on the beach.

The pendulum cast

Pendulum casting is a group of styles which feature a preliminary swing of the sinker. Some casters use a huge arc, others cast big distances with a more abbreviated swing. Everyone's style must be built on fundamental rules that have little to do with personal preferences. From the mechanical point of view there are some things you can do with a pendulum cast, and some that will not work however much you practise.

Success depends on proper alignment of rod with sinker and leader. Unless they follow each other along the correct path the rod will not react properly and the cast will fly out of control. Controlled swing is one secret of pendulum technique. The spot in mid-air where the sinker peaks on its backswing determines the success or failure of the whole venture, and the trick is to discover exactly where the weight must be for you. Most casters find it by trial and error but you can save hours of frustration by going about it more logically.

The cast itself is an anticlimax. Copy what you did in the previous exercises, this time over a longer arc and with the additional boost of body power. Unwind your body, transfer weight from right leg to left then flick the rod handle over with that same powerful, smooth punch and pull. A powerful cast will put you on your toes, and you may even have to take a half step forward to preserve balance. The right arm is high, punched at roughly 45 degrees. The left pulls down to the bottom left-hand corner of your rib cage. The rod

Study the illustrations and in your mind's eye trace the line of the rod's tip

Pendulum swing

Sinker suspended on long drop; rod held almost vertical.

Outswing (away from water) to Position A.

Inswing (towards water).

Sinker at maximum height. 'Lost' sensation triggers the start of the power action. Position B.

Full power on the pendulum cast.

timing and control that few anglers could ever hope to achieve. But there is an easier option: in accordance with the laws of physics, any sinker lying inside the rod arc will tend to align itself with the rod tip when power is applied. Knowing that, we can write the golden rule of pendulum casting: when the main power stroke begins, the sinker must be *inside* the rod's arc and *above* the height of the tip ring.

Get into your starting position which should be similar to that illustrated. Check the sinker drop (around eight feet with an $11\frac{1}{2}$ foot surf blank and 5oz), flip the reel out of gear and hold the rod upright so that the sinker lies fairly close to the blank.

Flick the sinker away from you by dropping the rod tip away from the sea. Do not force the pace, but try to achieve reasonable power to take the sinker well outside the tip ring. When the sinker reaches maximum height on this outswing, reverse its direction with a strong, smooth, downward push with your left hand. Done properly this generates enough speed and momentum to sweep the sinker past the blank and out of sight past your right shoulder into Position B.

As the inswing drifts towards its maximum height you will sense a distinct feeling of 'losing' the sinker. (When the sinker climbs past your right shoulder, leader pressure drops just enough to give the sensation that the sinker has suddenly disappeared.) That feeling triggers the main power stroke of the cast. Turn your head and look up into the air where you want the cast to go. Shoulders will follow automatically, and the cast finishes with the same javelin-like pull through and arm action used in the off-ground style.

ring as it powers through a big cast. The sinker swings out to Position A, back in a pendulum arc to Position B, then follows the rod tip through its main power stroke. As the rod accelerates the leader and sinker must be properly aligned along the aerial pathway.

A sinker's position at the end of its pendulum inswing (Position B) therefore determines whether the cast will be good or bad. In theory you should develop a technique that perfectly aligns the leader and sinker. In practice that calls for a degree of

4 Rigs and tactics

Basic tactics

Everyone's first attempts at shore fishing are rather clumsy. Casts fly left and right, tackle refuses to anchor in the tide, baits tear from the hook in mid-cast. You do not even know exactly when to strike the bite. Go to an open, uncrowded stretch of seashore and take life as it comes. If you have an experienced angler to point you in the right direction, so much the better. But you can avoid the major pitfalls just by reading about rigs, baits and tackle assembly. Those and casting probably account for most early headaches. Legering catches more fish than all other methods combined because most fish hooked from open beaches, surf, estuaries and rocks are bottom feeders that prefer natural baits like worms, crabs and fish. Make learning to use a leger your priority, then you can fish 99 per cent of the British coastline with confidence.

Open beaches

Competent anglers can easily fish close together but it takes just one who does not cast straight to ruin the day for everyone else. It is a nightmare to fish next to someone who casts over your line or whose tackle drifts in the current and tangles with a dozen others. Find yourself a spot at least fifty yards away from the next man and avoid the problem of casts that escape a little too late or early and fly astray. As long as you use a grip wired lead, your tackle will not drift too far out of control.

A reasonably flat beach with no offshore obstructions to trap the terminal rig and line is much easier to fish than rocks and rough ground. Even if your local coastline is predominantly rocky, choose a clean

Skilled anglers can easily fish side by side, but beginners need at least fifty yards between themselves and the next man.

Simple paternoster with snood tied eighteen inches above the sinker.

beach for your first attempts. At least you will not fall down the cliff while you struggle to master the rod and reel.

Terminal rig principles

Terminal rigs are systems of presenting baits so that fish find them easily and are encouraged to attack. Location and attraction are the overriding considerations. The object is to present the bait in the right place at the right time. Provided that bait is well chosen, the chances of a bite are excellent. Water conditions and the way fish feed dictate the design of terminal rigs. Sometimes baits must lie in place long enough for fish to find them. Static rigs cast from the beach catch a broad cross-section of fish, from dabs to conger eels. If you can locate the ideal spot on the sea-bed, legering is the perfect answer to bottom fishing because it is easy to control, highly effective and economical in tackle.

Sometimes an anchored bait is attacked and swallowed without hesitation, in which case fixed traces work adequately. Now and again the fish creeps up and plays with the bait. Unless the rig is constructed to give the fish plenty of leeway in the form of slack line, a bite never develops. Paternosters are inferior to a running leger in that respect. Learn to design and handle both rigs; they cover so many aspects of beach fishing and catch so many species of fish that you cannot afford to overlook either.

Paternosters

Paternoster construction is very simple. The sinker is attached to the very end of your line with the sinker knot protected from sea-bed abrasion by a split ring or a swivel. One, two or three hooks on short traces called snoods are spaced along the central rib of the paternoster. You can buy outriggers to support snoods and hooks but most anglers opt for stand-off loops tied directly into the main rib, or better still a tough, swivelling nylon boom like the Avis device.

Paternosters can be tied directly in the main reel line or casting leader but are better made detachable. Join the rig to the shock leader with a split ring, swivel or

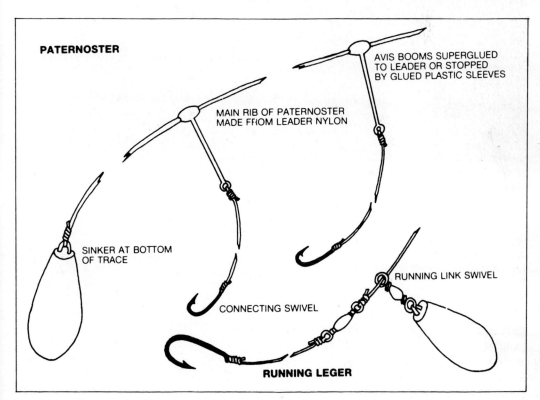

Beach trace design principles.

39

quick-fastening clip. You can store dozens of spare rigs in a plastic bag, so there is no need to waste time tying a new one should the original snap off in casting or foul on the sea-bed. *Important*: the central rib of a detachable paternoster must be of a breaking strain equal to or higher than that of the casting leader. Otherwise it snaps first cast.

The exact dimensions of a paternoster are seldom critical and will be explained in later chapters. As a rule, use a number of hooks appropriate to the size of fish and strength of rod and reel. It is no good hooking three conger eels at once; on the other hand why waste time catching whiting on a one hook rig when you could just as easily haul them out two or three a cast?

Paternosters are useful for catching mackerel and other species attracted to artificial lures. A string of feathered snoods or bright strands of silver foil catch mackerel by the score. Four to six hooks are a neat balance between easy control and rapid results. Feathers backed up by natural baits, usually strips of mackerel, and jigged close to the bottom lure most species of fish.

Running legers

One hook mounted below a sinker sliding freely on the shock leader is the preferred rig for shy species and a better means of fishing big single baits. Construction is very easy, and as the diagrams illustrate you can choose the length of trace best suited to the species you aim to catch. Wire and monofilament traces between six inches and six feet long are equally well accommodated.

Running legers are fished static or slowly rolling across the sea-bed. Movement of the rig itself or pressure of tide against the main line of an anchored rig reduces the free-running properties. Unless the main line is relatively slack, a fish cannot move off with the trace without disturbing the sinker. When that is the case you may as well use a single hook paternoster. However, on the whole the running leger works well enough to merit serious attention. Like the paternoster it is useful for all-round bottom fishing for the majority of fish. It excels for tope, conger eels, and rays that live in deep water close to rocks, piers and harbour walls.

Breakaway sinker, armed (left) and released (right).

When you see or feel a definite bite, pick up the rod, wind down hard, then lift the rod tip to maintain tension.

Setting up

As far as possible set up your tackle at home. Make up two or three double hook paternosters and carry them to the beach in individual plastic bags. You could tie on the snooded hooks when you make up the rest of the rig, but it is neater to carry them separately. Tying them on the beach leaves you free to choose the right size hook for the day's conditions and baits.

Two sizes of hooks should accommodate most of your early fishing: size 2–1/0 for general fishing, and size 4/0–6/0 for cod and

the other bigger species. Aberdeen eyed hooks are excellent in both cases. Use 15lb snoods on the smaller hooks, 20–25lb on the larger. Snoods of 18in are a handy length; you can soon cut them down if necessary.

Find your place on the beach, park your tackle well back from the water's edge and set up your rod rest. Push the two sections of rod tightly together with the rings lined up from tip to butt. Attach the reel and make sure the winch fitting is screwed down comfortably secure.

Clip a 5oz sinker on the paternoster's

Hard-biting cod in fast water invariably hook themselves. Most beach species follow that trend.

lower swivel or split ring. Make sure it is absolutely secure to withstand hard casting. Wired bombs of all types are satisfactory, but the Breakaway sinker available at most tackle shops is a favourite for routine beach fishing. Check that the swivelling wires are trapped by beads which slot into grooves in the lead. If the beads spring out prematurely, tackle drifts out of control.

Tie on two snooded hooks. Flat-fish, whiting, school bass, codling and silver eels – common species to catch from the

beach – are easily hooked on small Aberdeens. Small hooks are usually more productive when you are fishing for anything that comes along. Save the bigger hooks until you know there are winter cod or specimen bass hunting the shallows.

Local preferences dictate your choice of baits. Most whiting, codling, bass and flatfish are hooked on worms of some description. But do ask at the tackle shop and see what other anglers on the beach use for bait. It may be that sand-eels, fish strips or crabs are essential. Check first, then you will know exactly what to put on the trace. If in doubt stick to worms: lug in winter, ragworms in summer.

Tackle control

Most beaches are swept by tidal currents powerful enough to drag sinker and line downstream. Sometimes it pays to drift the bait but on the whole a static rig hooks more fish. Grip wires on the sinker boost anchorage only if the angle of the line is correct in relation to the current. The worst mistake is to recover slack line immediately after the cast lands in the water. Instead, let go another 10–25 yards of line. The extra bow of nylon improves the sinker's efficiency and makes it dig hard into the sea-bed. Now prop your rod in the rest and wait for a bite.

Bites

Hungry fish bite hard enough to signal a clear reaction at the rod tip. Even dabs 150 yards away in rough water are easily detected. Most sea fish take the bait so eagerly they hook themselves. The trace snaps tight against the inertia of the grip sinker and drives the barb home. Striking in the accepted sense is unnecessary. Watch for a distinct and continuing reaction on the rod tip, pick up the rod and wind in until you feel resistance. Then raise the rod tip as high as you can reach and *hold the tension*. The worst mistake is to let the line go slack.

Sometimes a bite is so fierce that the sinker loses its grip. Line falls slack before you pick up the rod. Wind as fast as you can until you feel the weight of the fish, then lift the rod to maintain pressure. Reel the fish gently ashore; there is no need to rush: well hooked fish seldom escape. Pump the line if necessary: lift the rod, then drop the tip while winding back the slack line that results. Again lift the tip to haul back more line – drop the rod and turn the reel – lift the rod again. Pumping is the smooth, efficient way to pull in a heavy fish without straining the tackle or your winding arm.

Guide the fish towards the shore, wait until a wave picks it up then make a final, smooth lift which hauls it clear of the water and dumps it on the sand. Grab the fish by the tail and carry it high and dry. Small species like whiting and flatties are simply cranked out of the water and swung ashore on the rod. Unhook your fish, rebait the tackle and cast again. When a shoal is within casting range you cannot afford to waste time admiring the catch.

Practice

Time spent practising legering and casting on open beaches is amply repaid when you progress to rocks, rough ground and crowded beaches. With your basic skills now second nature you can afford to spend more time on learning about baits, other kinds of terminal tackle, sea-bed and weather, and advanced casting techniques like the pendulum. You feel confident enough to mix with experienced anglers. You know how to tie the important rigs, how to present baits, how to stop line drifting across everyone else. There is a lot to learn, but as long as you get off on the right foot it is easy enough.

5 Whiting

The first whiting of the year bring summer fishing to a close and set the pace for long winter months of shore fishing. Whiting are an essential part of our sport, though in reality they have little enough to offer. Small, ravenous fish which invade every inch of the British coastline, they are amazingly easy to catch and therefore perfect for the newcomer. For all the commercial fishing, amateur netting and coastal pollution, whiting thrive where other fish suffer. Since cod fishing declined from the early 1960s glut, whiting have expanded to fill the vacuum.

Many species of fish prefer specific habitats and water depths. Whiting are happy in deep water over reefs and rocks, along open beaches of sand and shingle, in calm water and roaring surf. Though not particularly tolerant of low salinity they still infiltrate the upper reaches of estuaries.

Identification

The whiting is a member of the family that includes cod and pollack. It is a silvery fish, white bellied and greenish on the back with pearly scales which brush off at a touch. Like the cod it has a relatively large mouth with tiny, sharp teeth. At first glance you may confuse a small cod with a whiting but there are two tell-tale signs that separate the species. Whiting have no barbule under the chin; codling, no matter how small, possess a single barbule. There is a black spot at the base of the whiting's pectoral fin. Notice too that the whiting's eye is relatively much bigger. It is a less robust fish whose colours are really very different. Though exact shades and patterns vary in cod, whiting are uniformly immaculate, silvery fish which glow coral-pink in the autumn sunlight. Cod are drab by comparison, dirty on the belly, marbled back and flank.

Habits

The whiting's annual cycle steers massive shoals into casting range sometime during the middle weeks of September. Sometimes they move in earlier; other years the earliest fish show in October. But you can depend on their arriving at some stage. Then shore fishing changes into top gear. Anglers who never bother to cast a line all summer head for the beach. Tackle shops do a roaring trade with lugworms, tackle and mackerel baits.

Most whiting hooked are migrants; there are also a few small shoals that hang around deep water all year and which, like pouting and the occasional out-of-season codling, may show any time. The whiting that interest us are the annual visitors which outnumber the rest a million to one. When the main shoals arrive you should be hauling them out by the dozens. Thirty or forty fish is good going but unlikely to set the world alight. Even a moderately successful trip in October–November should produce fifteen or twenty fish a rod.

Early season whiting bite better after dark. In mid-September, expect to hook little or nothing during the day and only a few fish at night. Daylight catches may be respectable by the middle of October, but the bulk of whiting are still hooked after dusk. The ratio of night to day whiting holds steady at five or more to one and may be far higher in the calm, bright days of late autumn when the sea lies glass-smooth. The basic rule is to fish at night whenever you can. Failing that, concen- trate on late afternoon tides.

Tides

Whiting arrive inshore on some of the big- gest tides of the year, the autumn equinox springs. The rush of water, its associated rough weather and a tailing off in water temperature flush summer away and en- courage the sea-bed to close down for the coming winter. Falling air temperatures and shorter days accelerate the process. Big tides are the turning point of the year,

The late autumn run of whiting draws thousands of anglers to the beach.

a brief period between easy living summer and harsh reality of winter and they herald the beginning of the whiting season proper.

Tides are perhaps less a factor in fishing for whiting than for cod or bass. Whereas the bigger species tend to swim and feed to a tidal pattern, whiting are less fussy. Bass and cod switch on and off; whiting merely vary their feeding rate. The two hours each side of high water are universally successful and high water itself produces plenty of bites; far from the case with

Night fishing produces far better catches. The whiting grabbed mackerel bait, while the dab on the lower paternoster took lugworm.

many other species, which tend to slow down or stop feeding during that brief spell of static water.

Tide, then, influences the number of whiting willing to feed at any given time but is seldom a make or break factor. The classic whiting tide is midway between neaps and springs with high water around 8 p.m. in late October. Sheer numbers of whiting override any criticism of their sporting merit. On very light tackle they fight hard enough, but any fish that weighs less than two pounds is hardly in the 'Jaws' class. It is the certainty and ease of whiting fishing that counts. No fish provides a beginner with such a mighty boost in confidence. On your first trip to sea or beach you could easily land a dozen prime fish. There cannot be a better introduction to the sport. It certainly beats waiting six months for your first bass.

Baits and rigs

Whiting feed on or close to the sea-bed. Not a fussy creature by any means, it eats crabs, worms and small fish including smaller whiting. Shrimps are snapped up in vast numbers; early winter fish hooked from open beaches are sometimes full to overflowing. Lugworms and fresh fish baits account for the majority of whiting. Ragworms, sand-eels and peeler crab work well but prove too expensive when shoals are biting fast and furious. Two pounds of fresh herring or mackerel cost less than a quarter pound of ragworms and usually outfish them anyway, so why waste money?

To some extent lugworms are therefore unnecessary; indeed if anything, whiting attack fish more readily. Yet there is always the chance of cod turning up, and

Fresh frozen mackerel cut into 'commas'.

they certainly do take lugworms in preference to fish. Thus with all-round prospects in mind, you might choose a cocktail bait of lugworm tipped with fish strip. It covers the options and spins out those expensive worms.

Buy your mackerel (herrings if you can find a supply) in deep-frozen blocks. Order several pounds at a time because the price is more competitive and you are sure of adequate freshness. Order a box from your local fishmonger, visit the fish market or wait on the quayside for a commercial boat to come in with the day's catch. An even better plan is to feather a freezer-load of mackerel in summer and keep them specifically for the autumn whiting.

Though not as discriminating as, say, thornback rays, whiting are not enthralled by a chunk of greasy, soft mackerel which has been lurking on the slab for a week. Firm, bloody bait encourages more bites. Lay the whole fish on a board and cut it in back-to-belly chunks each half an inch wide. Work along the fish from head to tail. Flip each tiny cutlet face up, then slice it from top to bottom. The result is a comma shaped chunk of flesh full of blood and oil, supported by a tough rind of skin. Each piece is the ideal size for whiting, and you waste none of the mackerel – even the head cuts down into attractive baits. Treat herrings the same way.

Hook size is less important than with most species but it pays to keep to a minimum. Size 4–2/0 fine wire Aberdeens, well sharpened, penetrate easily whatever the casting distance. You may find that too small a bend slides far into the whiting's throat, in which case step up a couple of sizes in the interests of conservation. The millions of whiting are still no excuse for killing fish unnecessarily.

Cocktails of mackerel and lugworm are economical and effective. Sometimes the bait appeals more if the lugworm goes on second and hangs down from the bend. The disadvantage is that during a hard cast the weight of the fish chunk pushes the worm off the hook. Mounted the other way around, the fish acts as a soft bed for the worm. By nicking the point and bend of the hook through the skin rather than directly into the flesh, you can be sure that

Small but sharp teeth abrade nylon snoods. Change the line when it feels rough.

the bait casts reliably and better withstands crab attack.

Shrimps score top marks with whiting fishermen. A live shrimp is all but impossible to cast on conventional terminal tackle because it rips from the hook under the lightest acceleration. Frozen shrimps cast better but are messy. Some fishermen bait the hook, then freeze it solid. Every cast therefore requires its own trace, and each baited hook must be stored in a vacuum flask of ice. Overall it is hardly worth the effort even if shrimps are freely available.

The Baitsafe capsule is the solution. Catch live shrimps and store them in a bucket of water or in damp weed in a cooler box. Use a small, fine wire hook like the Aberdeen Blue inserted once through the shrimp's back. Pack the trace in the Baitsafe and cast as hard as you like: safe inside its plastic box a shrimp stays intact over the longest distances.

The disadvantages of Baitsafes – one reason why matchmen shy away – is the restriction to one hook. You can cram two baits into the capsule, but it never works too well. Whiting fishing is traditionally the realm of the two and three hook paternoster. When the fish are biting well, expect to land a full house.

Cut a four foot piece of leader, tie a split ring top and bottom for line and sinker attachment then tie in two or three standoff loops or Avis booms. Add bait clips for long distance work. Six to twelve inch snoods are plenty long enough, and within reason the breaking strain is immaterial. Even stiff snoods do not deter a whiting. On the other hand, avoid snoods under 10lb test unless you check for nylon abrasion after every fish. Whiting have small but sharp teeth which scour the line next to the hook.

Tactics

The whiting invasion triggers an annual renewal of interest in beach fishing. But the magic soon dulls. Two or three good sessions on the beach, up to your neck in whiting, fingers skinned from their rough teeth, and you would rather call it a day. As sporting fish whiting are a non-event. All right, they win matches and are so easy to catch that newcomers score on their first ever trip to the seashore. Is that all the species has to offer? It is if you stick to conventional beach tackle. Ordinary tackle is important of course. Sometimes you need the momentum of a 4–6oz sinker to drive baits far enough and to anchor them in a fast flood current. Pendulum rods, fixed spool reels and multipliers are an essential feature of autumn beach fishing.

Later in the year and through until next spring, cod figure higher and higher in your list of priorities. Winter winds, powerful tides and rough water impose their own restrictions on tackle selection, so there is no point buying a lightweight rod as the mainstream weapon in your armoury. From the all-round shorefishing viewpoint, as opposed to specialised angling for whiting, a standard 5–6oz outfit is the better investment.

Now suppose you are several years into the sport. Although you look forward to the whiting if only as an excuse to remind yourself what it is like to hook fish cast after cast, the exercise soon pales. Six weeks into the new season you are fed up with the wretched things.

There are at least two avenues to explore. Lighter, more sporting tackle allows whiting enough breathing space to put up a bit of fight. Artificial lures really are a viable alternative to natural baits. You

Specimen two pound whiting from Orford Island, Suffolk.

these rods toss baits plenty far enough. Such light tackle is restricted by waves and weather but it is far tougher than most sea anglers realise. When tidal current dies at low and high water an ordinary drilled bullet or swivelled $\frac{3}{4}$–$1\frac{1}{2}$oz bomb either holds its ground or drifts slowly. Often you can trigger an attack by inching the bait along the sea-bed. Dabs and flounders too are suckers for this treatment. At the highest flow of ebb and flood, switch to a miniature grip lead or Breakaway bomb weighing 1–3oz. Two ounce makes a handy combination with the six pound line: tackle holds steady at 100 yards or can be drifted by pumping the rod every minute or two.

The terminal rig for light line whiting is either a running leger with the hook on a 12–18 inch trace of 10lb line or a single hook paternoster with snoods under nine inches. Exact dimensions are not important and it does not matter if the paternoster has one or more hooks. The aim is to wring the last ounce of fight from an individual fish, not to fill the freezer.

Whiting are ferocious little predators that spend less time scavenging than cod do. The shoals do chase their prey along the ground and in the layers of water just above the bottom, hunting by taste and smell, but they are equally geared to locating midwater meals by sight and vibration. Artificial lures are therefore potentially as good as legered natural baits.

Deep, fairly clean water at short range, falling light and actively feeding fish in tight shoals are the scenario for spinning and jigging. Toby, German sprat, spoons and Vibro lures catch whiting; feathers are excellent and slowly spun live sand-eel is devastating. Use light tackle and a selec-

catch fewer fish perhaps, but they are fun – no comparison to the sluggish creature hauled out on normal casting tackle.

Variations

Autumn brings its share of still days when the sea cannot raise a tickle of surf. Onward of the last hour of daylight, whiting shoals creep within 30 yards of steep shingle beaches and rock marks. Carp/pike tackle is more than adequate. With 6lb line, fixed spool reel and an ounce of lead

*Groynes and breakwaters shelter small fish and shrimps which
hungry whiting attack day and night.*

tion of lures worked erratically. Even a
12oz fish hits very hard indeed. Hooked on
sub-10lb class tackle, it is a very different animal from the same size whiting dragged
ashore on the usual beach equipment.

6 Flounders and dabs

Flounders

Flounders save the day for matchmen and pleasure anglers. Along with whiting these flat-fish form the backbone of shore fishing in Britain. An undemanding fish to catch, always hungry, living in estuaries and along the open coast, the flounder is a lot of fun even if it is one of the muddiest-tasting creatures in the sea.

Flounders are broadly similar to dabs. If you were to lay the species side by side the differences would be obvious, whereas an isolated fish hooked from the beach may create problems. The flounder is a burly fish compared to the dab. Dabs smell sweet but flounders usually stink. The shape of the lateral line is an instant clue: the flounder's is fairly straight, the dab's arches behind the gill cover. Brush your finger over the fish's back from tail to head. Scales on a flounder feel smooth whereas the dab's are distinctly rougher. Look on the head as well: flounders grow a patch of very rough, raised scales. The dab is featureless. Flounders weigh 8oz to 2lb on average. Any dab over 8oz is worth having; a one pounder is huge for most beaches and the rare 2lb fish is a prize winner.

Flounders and plaice are closely related and may even cross breed. That does create identification problems. The spots on a plaice are a vivid red which remain long after the fish is taken from the sea. A flounder's spots are duller red and fade rapidly. Some flounders do not have spots anyway. On the whole though, spots are a fairly reliable guide to species.

The back of a plaice's head shows a row of distinct raised lumps called tubercles. The overall shape of the fish is broader and slightly more circular-looking than a flounder's. A flounder's fins seem angular compared to the softly contoured fins of a plaice. Just in front of the flounder's anal fin protrudes a sharp spike which although not unique to the species is very well developed. It is an offshoot of the vertebral column, not a fin ray.

Habits

Flounders spend much of their time close inshore feeding on crustaceans, small fish and whatever else can be rooted from the sea-bed. They certainly are not fussy eaters. The annual breeding cycle takes them seaward between Christmas and April. Exact seasons seem to vary with location and water temperature but in all cases the aim is the same: flounder eggs require precise salinity concentrations which are found well offshore. The annual trek of millions of flounders from estuaries and beaches is directed at providing the right start in life for their offspring. Otherwise they prefer to be close to land.

Flounders are an all-weather species which you can hook at the height of summer and in the coldest frost except when very rough seas modify their behaviour to

*Shallow, muddy ground along the Thames estuary is typical of
the best flounder marks.*

some extent. Wildly churning waves deter them from swimming within easy casting range and kill their appetite. Above all they try to avoid water clouded with swirling sand and silt, although much depends on the clarity of the normal environment. Flounders brought up on clean Atlantic beaches are much fussier than those resident in permanently grubby estuary tides.

Tactics

Water clarity, wave action and depth are important aspects of open-beach flounder fishing. Casting distance is linked to the flounder's pattern of feeding, so for best results learn to work in step with the fish. Sometimes you need to reverse the operation to avoid them, for they are a nuisance if your target is bass. As the tide rises from dead low water, bass move quickly on to the shallows and into the breaking surf. Flounders are far slower to swim in. If you aim to hook bass, cast short. For flounders, blast the bait beyond the lines of surf. Towards high tide, flounders move up to join the bass. Casts of 50–75 yards usually do the trick. Soon after the beginning of

A double hook paternoster baited with ragworms or crabs – standard tackle for match and pleasure angling.

main foreshore slope. Avoid treading on a flounder as you wade to cast.

Surf beaches and shingle banks provide good flounder fishing throughout the year; expect to hook them on most baits and bottom-fished rigs. Elsewhere the odd flounder is likely to turn up any time whether you fish for them specifically or for codling, dabs, bass, dogfish and whiting. In most circumstances outside of match fishing it is probably not worth fishing for them exclusively anyway. Even so, they are an important species that no serious beach fisherman should ignore.

During the winter spawning migration, at its peak between December and March, flounders concentrate in the lower reaches of major river systems and in minor estuaries and saltwater inlets. Sheltered waters like the Thames, Blackwater and Humber, the Solent and Poole Harbour (indeed all natural and man-made harbours) support massive shoals of flatties. Catches of fifty fish a rod are not unknown.

Baits and tackle

Flounders prefer meaty baits. Lugworms, ragworms, fish, sand-eels and crabs are snapped up. Peeler and soft crabs probably head the list of specialist flounder baits, closely followed by lively sand-eels and absolutely fresh herring strips. White and harbour ragworms are extremely good baits, and if all else fails lug and mackerel do well enough. Matchmen insist on the finest baits because a high percentage of beach matches are won or lost purely on flounders. The pressures are nowhere so great for pleasure fishing, so the secondary baits may well suffice for the occasional bash.

the main ebb run, flounders creep away while faster-moving bass, which rely on their speed to prevent being stranded, linger inshore. Go back to the original plan: cast short for bass, long for flounders.

Elsewhere the pattern is more obscure but as a basis for experiment it pays to cast long at low water and progressively shorten the range as the tide floods to maximum depth. Sometimes it is better to cast only 25 yards while flounders feed in the gully between the upper beach and the

Two and three hook paternosters are excellent for general bottom fishing and permit hard casting when necessary. Flounders are often caught at short–medium range, but there are occasions when absolute distance pays off: you may want to stay in contact with a gully or creek as the tide forces you back up the beach. Short snoods tied direct to stand-off loops are spaced 18in apart along the centre rib of the paternoster. Nine inch snoods of 15lb monofilament are adequate. No flounder can break even 6lb line on a direct pull, but you have to contend with its

Harbour ragworm bait.

sharp teeth grinding the line just above the hook. A string of flatties caught on the same hook soon reduce the trace breaking strain.

Flounders are unpalatable so the majority of anglers throw them back, sizeable or not. Unhooking flounders is a real problem because they take the hook deep. Forceps sometimes wriggle the bend free but they do not work if the shank is right down to the base of the stomach. Small flatties are adept at gulping the hook completely beyond reach.

Small, fine wire hooks are one answer. Blue Aberdeens in the size 2–2/0 range are plenty big enough to hold the bait and strong enough to land big fish – even a cod if you hook one – but the wire is soft and pliable. Hold the fish across its back, pull on the trace until you feel the hook begin to straighten deep inside the fish's throat, then smoothly and quickly increase pressure until the barb pulls free. It sounds a brutal exercise but is far kinder than forceps. Afterwards, reform the hook bend with pliers. You can straighten an Aberdeen at least half a dozen times before the metal is seriously weakened.

Sinker weight depends on the fishing ground. Calm water and modest tides allow 1–3oz rigs with appropriately light rods, lines and reels. Where distance is not important, as in habour wall floundering, try a carp/pike outfit and 6lb line. Elsewhere, bass-grade tackle is excellent. Unfortunately many of the better flounder marks are swept by powerful tides. Big rivers push aside 5oz tackle and you may be forced to use 8oz of lead even at close range. However, as a rule you can fish 4–6oz with ease from most estuary banks and beaches except on springs.

Tactics

If the flounders are running and feeding hard, simply cast out and wait for a bite. At the height of the season you can afford to leave the first fish out there while other flounders attack. Three hook paternosters often produce a full house. The bite is both positive and powerful, and flounders hook themselves against the inertia of the sinker. Match anglers used to kill every flounder they landed. At the end of a big competition hundreds of dead fish were tossed into the sea for the gulls. Today's conservation-minded anglers protect the catch in a bucket of fresh sea water. Flounders lie quiet all day and provided you keep them out of direct sunlight and heat they survive to bite another day.

Atlantic surf beaches are excellent for flounders. Sometimes the entire beach is alive; more often shoals concentrate where freshwater flows over the sand. Small estuaries and streams are the hottest spots of all. Ordinary flounder techniques and baits work well though distance might

There is no finer species than flounders for teaching the basics of beach fishing.

pay off more than on other beaches. Cast your bait well behind the breaking surf where the water is deeper and mutes the effects of the churning waves. The advantage of surf beaches is their lack of strong cross currents. Replace your grip wired sinker with a plain bomb. Let it roll the bait along the sea-bed. If it stays put, pull the rod tip around every five minutes and take in the slack.

Work the bait across the sand in short jumps. Flounders home in on spurts of sand thrown up by the sinker, which they confuse with crab or sand-eel activity. Investigating the puff of sand, the hunting flounder pounces on your bait. It is a simple trick which pays off time after time. A couple of bright beads above the bait or a small spinner of silver foil mounted on the snood definitely does produce more bites than a plain bait.

Dabs

Hooked dabs do not exactly set the world alight. They bite hard but are incapable of testing even a spinning outfit. Why do so many beach anglers fish for them? Because they are dependable fish which taste at least as good as soles and plaice. Many anglers rate them the finest eating fish in the sea.

There is a rough parallel between the best times to fish for dabs and the peak months of the cod season. If cod are around in significant numbers, few anglers bother to chase dabs. Yet as soon as cod move away, even temporarily as they do around Christmas, dabs are suddenly a favourite target. During those codless weeks of the New Year, a bag of flatties brightens your day on the beach. There is another link between dabs and cod, especially along the east and south-east coasts. The dab population expands in poor cod seasons and the fish themselves grow heavier. Dabs probably figure high on an inshore cod's menu, which explains the see-saw balance between the two species.

Habits

Dabs are widely spread throughout the British Isles and like flounders they turn up all year. Almost everywhere the best fishing lies between October and April. Sometimes the peak time lasts for no more than six weeks, usually in the depths of winter. Unlike flounders they are intolerant of low salinity and prefer to live on an open coast unaffected by freshwater contamination. Much depends on the depth and area of an estuary: some deep, short inlets with little drainage capacity do attract lots of dabs. For most beach anglers though, it pays to fish the exposed open-sea beaches and rocks.

Clean sea-beds with a scattering of sand, hardpacked mud and shingle are better dab marks than soft, oozing mud. Rocks and weed beds sometimes produce good hauls, but most heavier bags are caught on open beaches. Time and tide often make no difference. Daylight fishing continues to be excellent even in bright sunlight and a calm sea. Top and bottom water fish well, but sport usually slackens at the strongest flow of ebb and flood tide especially on big springs.

Dabs are essentially bottom-feeders but they are by no means slow moving. Most of their food – small fish, worms, crabs and shrimps – lives on or close to the sea-bed. Sometimes dabs lie in wait, half covered by sand, but more often they quarter the

The dab, sporting and full of flavour, a favourite with beach fishermen throughout Britain.

yards away, there is not a fish from one week to the next. For some reason shoals of dabs feed between two or three groynes on a half-mile strip of apparently uniform beach but are seldom if ever hooked between any of the other breakwaters. Trial and error fishing is better than nothing: if you fish for half an hour without landing a dab, move 100 yards and try again.

Tactics

On average it pays to cast short. On beaches where an inshore gully is backed by a shallow sand-bar at, say, 100 yard range there might well be a case for long distance casting if fish concentrate on the bank itself. Explore the near and far slopes of the bank plus the inshore gully. But remember that the strip of sand just beyond the breakers is equally attractive to these little fish. Many if not most fine dabs are hooked within 50 yards of the rod tip.

Small hooks rigged on a simple paternoster are a fine rig for all-round beach fishing for dabs, whiting and codling which often make up a mixed catch from a winter beach. The trick is to balance bait and hook size. Cod-size hooks are too big for dabs. Very fine wire flatty hooks tend to lose their grip on a cod's jaws. Size 4–1/0 blue Aberdeen hooks are excellent for dabs, handle whiting easily enough and give you a fair chance with cod. Size 2–1/0 Patridge MW are a neat balance between precision and power. Fine enough in the wire, razor sharp and small enough to handle dabs, they are still more than strong enough to land a 10lb cod. The neat eye does not burst small lugworms either.

beach in search of a meal. Consequently, moving baits are sometimes far better than legered baits.

Even if they are not highly influenced by time and tide, dabs certainly do feed to a pattern which varies between beaches. Sometimes you pick up a steady stream of flatties throughout the day or night. More often they feed in spurts: you hook half a dozen fish in an hour then wait ages for the next shoal. Nor is an entire beach hunted by dabs. Some channels, gullies and sandbanks attract and hold masses of dabs; fifty

Dabs often feed just behind the backwash where waves swill food from the sea-bed.

Baits

Lugworms, white ragworms, harbour rag, slivers of fresh fish and small chunks of sand-eel are classic dab baits. Hermit and peeler crab are excellent as well. Of them all, lugworms take some beating and this is one case when second-rate baits sometimes hook more fish. When lugworms get old they either blow up and soften or shrivel into black strips as tough as liquorice. Either way they stink. Smell attracts dabs by the score. Thread a small bunch of shrivelled worms on the hook or pour on the runny kind. If necessary tip the bait with a small fresh lug or a sliver of fish to support the soft stuff for hard casting. If you do not need to throw a long way – and mostly with dabs you should limit your range – that buffer is not essential. Even semi-liquid lugworms should travel fifty yards without help.

It makes more sense to use light tackle than to heave out dabs on a standard beachcaster outfit. Sometimes you can fish just an ounce or two of lead on a spinning rod and 8lb line. In bad conditions you need the extra power and weight

of a normal beach rod and reel matched to 5–6oz of lead. In extremes of winter, ultra-heavy tackle is necessary to beat tide and waves. Dabs keep right on feeding in the teeth of a gale. You may find they stick around when whiting and even cod move off.

(Opposite) A short snood paternoster armed with fine wire hooks takes care of routine dab fishing.

7 Cod

Cod are powerful fish easily caught on sporting tackle, and in good seasons they shoal hundreds strong on almost every inch of the coastline. Without them sea fishing would nosedive into oblivion. Closely related to pollack, coalfish and haddock, cod are essentially a cold water species distributed from the North Polar region to well south of the English Channel. There are many races of cod, some resident, most migratory. The cod we catch are of the species *Gadus morrhua*, a fast-growing fish which moves into British waters in late October and stays to feed until early April.

The cod season begins with an autumn run of well conditioned fish of all sizes. October cod fall into the 3–7lb bracket along with enough double-figure fish to make life unpredictably pleasant. The cod season proper begins in November, peaks as the month runs into early December then settles down through the Christmas period.

Early January is disappointing because sprats and herrings preoccupy cod and draw them up from the sea-bed to feed in mid-water. In theory, cod fishing develops a second peak between February and early April. Sometimes it happens according to plan; more often these days sport gradu-ally dies off without a distinct recovery from the sprat invasion. The size of the spring cod varies considerably from that of the pre-Christmas peak. As well as produc-ing occasional fish in the 20lb bracket plus a fair run of 5–10lb codling, the sea is crammed with tiny codling less than nine inches long.

Northern waters never used to hold as many big fish as those in the south and south-east, but sheer numbers of codling compensated for any lack of twenty pounders. Newcastle and Hull, for exam-ple, produced more codling per angler than East Anglia and the south-east. The north-west, Wales and western Scottish Borders are less consistent but annually deliver a string of heavyweight specimens. In recent years these Atlantic-influenced areas have begun to take over from the traditional North Sea and Channel marks as all-round cod fisheries as well. At the moment it is difficult to predict what the long term trend may become.

Habits

A cod's aims in life are to breed and feed. Autumn/winter inshore migration triggers a feeding splurge which fattens the fish and boosts them into full breeding condi-

(Opposite) An excellent bag of whiting and cod. The big fish weighed 15lb, which is exceptionally good for most marks.

tion. Cod eat virtually anything that lives on the sea-bed, has died there or swims in mid-water. Even so, a cod's appetite does vary. It is wrong to assume that every cod in the sea sets its sights on a full belly and will settle for nothing less.

High levels of sea-bed food decrease the success rate of big baits, as if the cod were sick of gorging. In those conditions a small bait catches fish when a hookload lies neglected. The emphasis also switches from the traditional lugworm to white rag-worm, hermit crab and peeler shore crab.

Cod feed by sight, taste, feel and smell. In the dirty, fast-running tides that sweep the best cod marks, taste and smell are the major senses employed by hunting shoals. The scent trail exuded by a bait is vitally important. Too little scent washes away in the current and dilutes below the cod's sensory threshold. The key to bait selection lies more in scent content than in pure volume. Two or three small lugworms full of blood and juices cast into the water and changed before the sea destroys their scent trail always outfish half a dozen watery lugworms saturated by prolonged immersion.

Anglers who use tanked lugworms, which are notoriously low in natural scent, are forced to step up bait size to generate a sufficient trail. Six tanked worms are outgunned by two freshly dug lugworms. The traditional theory about big baits is a reflection of the balance between size and quality. Good baits for general codding do not need to be huge.

Stormy seas are an exception to the rule. When the sea swirls sand, foam and rub-bish through the tide, bait scents are blocked to some extent. More precisely, the scent lane fractures and is over-diluted. The only answer – and at best even this is second rate – is to increase the bait until it does throw out enough scent to produce an acceptable zone of attrac-tion. Big baits really do pay off in bad conditions: cod easily swallow half a dozen tough lugworms on an 8/0 long-shanked hook.

Smaller baits pay off in settled condi-tions. Cod are keen to take the easy pick-ings but, being well fed anyway, are less disposed to work hard for their dinner and seem reluctant to cover expanses of sea-bed to track down those elusive scents. A massive scent trail probably attracts more crabs, shrimps and flat-fish than it does cod. That alone wastes bait. You may as well stick to smaller baits which dabs and flounders find more manageable. Any cod that happens along will not pass up the opportunity for a snack, so either way you win.

In everyday fishing it comes down to this: if you must leave tackle out as long as possible in hard tides and rough weather, use big baits of the highest quality. Other-wise, thread on smaller baits and reload more often. Mixed species fishing – typi-cally taking pot luck with whiting, dabs, flounders and cod – favours the latter tech-nique. My own preference is smallish baits as routine unless the chances of a big cod are particularly high.

Baits

Lugworms merit star treatment because they are so widely used in cod fishing and, for the most part, produce the lion's share of the annual catch from the beach. Other baits are still valuable stand-bys and unbeatable when the going gets rough. Squid is the one bait which seems to dis-criminate between big and small fish of

The epitome of winter beach fishing. A pair of cod hooked on lugworm from Orford Island, Suffolk.

(Above) Genuine swell surf on an Atlantic bass beach. There was not a breath of wind.

(Left) An estuary lugworm bed where you can dig a hundred baits in half an hour. Most beds are far less prolific.

(Opposite) How it should be done — casting champion Paul Kerry in action.

The shore-caught record tope. A 57lb 2oz monster landed by Ray White in the West Country.

Mike Millman

Mike Millman

Inshore pollack are always much smaller than those hooked over the distant wrecks. A 5lb fish is a specimen.

(Above) A big shore-caught whiting by anybody's standards — a two pounder from the east coast.

(Left) Thornback ray landed from an Atlantic estuary.

(Opposite) A harbour wall where conger live in the crevices and feed on fish waste thrown from trawlers.

Shellgrit, sand, groynes and a scouring tidal effect add up to an excellent beach fishing mark for cod, whiting, flat-fish and even bass. Felixstowe, Suffolk.

Setting up camp for a long night's beach cod fishing. Comfort is the name of the game due to the long hours involved.

any species. Whole baby squid cast just behind the breakers of a steeply shelved beach – Chesil Beach is a favourite mark – takes an annual toll of 20lb-plus fish.

The fussiest cod nose along east coast beaches in spring. Lugworms are completely ignored, as are squid, mackerel, herring and the other back-up baits. White ragworms and peeler crab are the only baits that stave off disaster. Both are expensive in cash or in the time and distance required to collect them, but the investment is more than justified if you are serious about the sport.

Cod beaches

Shingle banks, estuary channels, mud/shell-grit and clean sandy foreshores are included on the extensive list of winter cod beaches. Dungeness beach, a deep, steeply shelved bank of sand and shingle swept by tide and winds, is worlds apart from the grubby banks of the Thames estuary at Gravesend and Tilbury. But both fish well for winter cod.

The essential features of an open-water cod beach lie beneath its surface. Sea-bed cover is negligible compared to the dense rock and weed kingdoms of North York-shire and Scottish cod. Open beaches rely more on fast tides and muddy water to encourage the cod to move inshore. Crabs, shrimps, worms and small bait fish lie behind boulders, beneath sand and mud, and in the shelter of gullies and sandbanks.

Cod gravitate towards rich feeding but their hunger is tempered with a healthy respect for their own skins. Calm water, good underwater visibility and slow currents discourage most bottom-feeding fish from swimming close inshore. Semi-darkness, vicious tidal currents and churn-

Big, juicy lugs are the most effective all-round cod bait.

ing waves boost a cod's confidence. Rough water also rakes the sea-bed and swills food creatures from their hiding places.

Deep water is far from essential for shore codding. Some of the finest beach marks in Britain hold less than 10 feet of water on a spring high tide. There are beaches that fish best on dead low tide with only 30 inches of dirty water. Generally though, modestly deep water (15–20 feet) produces more consistent sport and bigger fish. Shallow beaches normally fish badly in daylight but may transform after nightfall into the hottest spots on the coast.

Few beaches are truly featureless. Stones and weed patches speckle the foreshore; gullies and depressions intercut the sea-bed and provide cover and cross currents which attract and hold food. Make a point of surveying your local beaches at low water, preferably on big spring tides which strip the foreshore beyond casting range. Cod linger on weed beds and stony ground. They show a marked tendency to travel in gullies.

Tidal effect

Tides motivate cod's movements and feeding patterns. Dead high and low waters, without the pressure of tidal current, offer dull sport at best and may switch off the fish altogether. Strength of tide is far more important than its direction. Anglers still hold to the theory that flood outfishes ebb but long term statistics prove otherwise.

On the majority of open beaches swept by tides strong enough to attract cod within casting range, either flood or ebb proves better. Few beaches fish equally well on up and down tides. Even so, in peak season a beach that normally fishes better on the ebb may hold relatively more fish than

Still, bright conditions are not necessarily a deterrent if the water is deep and tidal currents run fiercely.

normal on the flood. Flood-preferred beaches demonstrate a similar pattern.

Expect variations within each rise and fall cycle. Most beaches have a distinct and often narrow period which outfishes the rest. Depending on the beach gradient, tidal force and the location of the beach in relation to offshore migratory routes and holding ground, cod feed on the first of the flood or ebb, in the middle of the tide, throughout a rise or fall, or for a brief spell both sides of top and bottom dead water. It is important to know how your local mark is most likely to fish – beaches ten miles apart may well prove opposites. If so, fish one beach on the flood, then shift marks for the ebb.

There is evidence that cod move along the coast in a saw tooth pattern rather than swim parallel to the tideline. This seems a particular feature of relatively shallow beaches protected by sandbanks. Cod move in and out through gullies cut into the sandy barrier. The habit reinforces the need to survey the beach at low tide. Frequent re-examination is necessary as well: a single winter storm generates enough power to shift sandbanks hundreds of yards and to rip out new channels.

Where a long, uniform beach shelves down on to hard-packed sand and mud, cod hunt along the base of the slope but are seldom evenly distributed along the entire length. At beach level the foreshore seems featureless, but from the air it is distinctly curved into a giant bay or a headland. Ordnance Survey maps and Admiralty charts provide the key to overall beach layout; although they are too imprecise to pinpoint the best marks individually they do indicate areas that repay closer investigation. Look for deeper water and a swirl of tide, both of which concentrate and hold food.

Bites

Full-blooded cod bites are easily recognised – the rod bounces, dives out of the rest or flips backwards in response to a slack line. The important consideration is that the bite you see on the rod tip is a reaction which travels up the line from the terminal rig; it always arrives after the event. By the time you see the bite the fish is either hooked or gone. Beyond the 75 yard range, striking is ineffective no matter how hard you thrash the rod. Instead, force the cod to hook itself against the inertia of a well anchored paternoster. If the hook is sharp, relatively fine in the wire and tethered close to the bottom by a grip lead, the momentum of the cod's attack drives home the barb.

The slack line bite is a result of the cod snatching the bait and trace so hard that the sinker wires lose their grip. It is the classic cod bite. Your only obligation is to reel in the slack line and tighten down on the fish before it has a chance to slip the hook. Cod are adept at spitting out a bait particularly if the hook skids on the tough skin around the jaw bones. Fine wire Aberdeen hooks are a step in the right direction though some are a little too soft in the wire for safety. Partridge Aberdeens and MW, Spearpoints and Vikings are excellent; Au Lion d'Or run them a close second with the Mustad standard Aberdeen ringed hooks only a little behind in strength.

Tactics

Cod fishing tactics depend on season and conditions. When cod are the prime target a single hook paternoster well baited with lugworms is an all-round favourite. Distance casting is usually important and may be the key factor. Any suitable outfit cast tolerably well should produce consistent 130 yard fishing distances. Do not worry too much if you can not manage 200 yard casts – a middle of the road 100–140 yards is far enough for satisfactory codding. By all means practise to improve your distances but do remember that there is far more to successful beach angling than merely blasting a bait to the horizon.

Where really big fish are likely to turn up, a mound of worms on the hook sometimes tips the balance in your favour. These days though, most fish run in the one to five pound bracket with only an isolated fish above ten pounds Rather than

(Opposite) A cod over five pounds is more than strong enough to rip the grip lead out of the sea-bed and produce the classic slack line bite.

stick with traditional cod hooks in the 4/0–8/0 range, try scaling down to 1/0–3/0 and never hesitate to cut down even more. Thread three or four medium lugworms along the hook and snood to produce a four to six inch column of bait. To reduce air resistance and bait damage during the cast, trap the hook against the leader with a casting clip and if necessary restrain the upper end of the bait with a nylon stop knot.

Cast as far into the tide as you can and make sure the grip wires on the sinker dig hard into the sea-bed. On the majority of open-beach cod marks you cannot afford to drift tackle around in the current: fishing distance drops; line tangles with other anglers' tackle. The secret of anchoring the weight is to let go an extra 15–25 yards of line after the sinker hits the water. A generous bow in the line sets the terminal rig at a more effective angle.

8 Rays and dogfish

Thornback rays

Thornbacks are the most widely distributed species of ray in British waters. Known also as roker they are predators that hunt the sea-bed for fish, worms and crustaceans. Except for the three species of true skate, the sting-ray and the blonde ray – all rare from the shore – the thornback is the heaviest member of the ray family likely to find itself on the end of a fisherman's line. Overall, the annual catch of thornbacks from beach and boat exceeds by a factor of at least five times the total number of other skates and rays. Hugely popular with anglers, the species is also important commercially. Chip shop 'skate' is actually thornback ray.

May and June usually see the peak of the rays' inshore migration. They come to breed, and it is their habit of grouping together on quite small areas of sandbanks and rough ground that makes them so vulnerable. Despite vicious commercial fishing pressure quite a few avoid the nets long enough for beach men to get a fair crack.

How close they come depends on depth of water, light intensity and weather. Deep water alongside cliffs and rocks entices fish to lie up and feed within spitting distance in all but stormy sea, and they usually feed some time during daylight hours. Thornbacks on shallower grounds spend most of their time way beyond casting range but do invade the beaches on a fairly regular basis in late evening and throughout the night. Sometimes they flap within 50 yards of the edge; usually you must blast a bait well past the 100 yards mark.

Tactics

Local pattern is a key factor particularly when the fish are few and far between. Few is the operative word these days: five or six sizeable beach thornies a season is good going. Times change and disappointment is guaranteed unless you set your sights somewhere within reason. On the other hand it is far from a doom and gloom situation. Get the basics right and you can score a time or two at least when the fishing hots up around late April.

The real skill of thornback fishing lies in working out the best spots. True of all fishing to some degree, with thornies it is the critical step in your campaign. Groups of rays never run the full length of a beach or sandbank system as, say, bass and cod may do. Nor like dabs and whiting do they invade the area in general. You cannot afford to cast in the wrong spot; often your bait must be within fifty yards of the hot-spot.

Though the trend for shallow water thornbacks is to lie in the shadow of sand-hills, on patches of semi-rough stones, weeds and coarse shingle, they still have particular likes and dislikes about exactly where to settle down and pair up. On my

71

local beach 90 per cent of the thornbacks are hooked in a 100 yard stretch of shell-grit and mud just downtide of a slight headland that diverts the flood current and creates an eddy. Nowhere else produces anything but the odd fish. The best you can do is watch other people and keep trying. And of course you can tap the local grapevine. What you cannot do – why, I don't know – is read the water as you might a cod or bass mark. With thornbacks, tradition and local knowledge are what count.

Deep water Atlantic marks fish differently from the shallow thornback grounds of the Channel, south and east coasts. The season is much longer, often continuing – though spasmodically – until late autumn storms and frosts drive the fish offshore. Rays take up residence close to the overhangs and weed beds. Male and female together, or small groups of breeding fish are the usual pattern. They are spread much more evenly than on shallow coastlines. If you catch one fish, another moves in to fill the gap. Like salmon in a river the newcomer takes up residence in the same spot, often within ten yards of where you hooked the first.

Locating rays and timing your attack calls for some skill. Catching them is something of an anticlimax. Assuming that your tackle is reasonably light (a 3ft trace of 25lb nylon carrying a 1/0–4/0 Viking or Spearpoint is about right from the beach) all you need concentrate on is the bait. Fresh is the operative word; and the basic menu includes crabs, herring, mackerel, sand-eels and sometimes ragworms.

The best bait depends on area. Deep, clean water leaves the options open but overall the vote must go to live sand-eel with peeler crab and mackerel close runners. Out in the sandbanks of the east coast and on shallowish beaches in general, mackerel and herring take a short lead from crabs. Sand-eel is a non-starter most of the time. Ragworms are the hot favourite on beaches where chances of a sting-ray are as good as, if not higher, than latching on to a thorny. A meaty king rag hedges your bets to some extent; but if you are stubborn enough to stick out for a thorny come what may, absolutely fresh herring gets the vote every time.

Smalleyed rays

British rays are basically alike. All species are far less common than the thornback from the general distribution point of view. However there are relatively few beaches and rock marks that produce thornback rays year after year. As commercial boats grab the lion's share of the annual inshore migration fewer fish remain for the beach man. Perhaps as a direct result we turn to other species, hence the popularity of smalleyed rays, now established as cult fish. It is hard to appreciate why they should be so popular, but down in the West Country and in Wales thousands of keen beach men make them first choice targets for spring to autumn fishing. Rock anglers catch most

(Opposite) Thornback ray – heaviest of the more common ray species.

A classic east coast thornback mark of sand, shell-grit and shallow, dirty water.

really are much smaller than you would expect to find on a thornback or any other British species of ray.

Habits

Occasional smalleyed rays turn up on Atlantic coasts throughout the year. The vast majority are hooked in deepish water from late spring to autumn. Cornwall, Wales, Ireland, the Channel Islands and parts of the Solent and Isle of Wight account for the most fish. Bigger specimens seem to turn up regularly from Jersey

Cutlets of frozen mackerel rigged on a single hook paternoster. The hook is strapped down with PVA tape.

smalleyed rays but that does not mean you never hook them from an open beach.

Smalleyed rays are smaller than thornbacks. A ten pounder is exceptional; most weigh between three and seven pounds. The fish is more delicately built than a thornback and lacks the pronounced thorns on wings and tail. It is dotted and patched with greens and browns over grey. Most fish have quite pronounced strips of white. The overall effect resembles streaks of paint. Indeed the fish is also known as the painted ray. Eyes are a give-away: they and Cornwall, perhaps because more anglers fish for them there.

Fairly settled weather, slight swell and overcast skies encourage rays inshore to feed in daylight. Fish are hooked between dawn and dusk, but many keen ray fishermen still prefer night-time. Beaches definitely fish better after dark probably because smalleyed rays are cautious about swimming into shallows flooded with sunlight. On the other hand perhaps feeding is easier at night. Rays are far from the fastest and most adept of hunters; they may find it better to creep up and pounce under

The smalleyed ray is lighter, more delicately built and prefers clean Atlantic water.

cover of darkness.

Tactics

Even from rocks with twenty feet or more of water within twenty-five yards, long range casting often pays off. Ray fishermen in Cornwall sometimes change down to six or eight pound line just to pick up the extra yards that carry baits right out into the tideway. It is seldom necessary to go to such extremes of breaking strain or distance but there is no doubt that pure casting performance often pays off, especially at the start and end of a season when there are fewer smalleyed rays along the coast and they are feeding sluggishly.

On open, sandy beaches a 75 yard lob drops a bait nicely behind the breakers. At the height of late summer/autumn surf fishing, the same cast could produce a bass or even a stray conger or tope. Where sandeels and crabs are the more popular baits, the odds on a specimen bass are much better than average. Ray anglers catch bass, and bass men hook smalleyed rays simply because the tactics, tackle and baits are almost identical.

Equipment

You need no special equipment for ray fishing. An ordinary beach outfit is excellent. If necessary, run-of-the-mill 5–6oz beachcasters can be rigged with light line to reach extreme range, but if you specialise in this technique look for a more progressive action in the blank. Matched to a fixed spool reel (much more efficient than a multiplier for light lines) a softer rod designed for 4–5oz easily outcasts conventional beach blanks.

Ordinary single hook traces are suitable

for ray fishing, both rock and surf. Wire is unnecessary and usually deters shy fish. A smalleyed ray's teeth are flat and blunt, certainly no match for even 20lb nylon. Specialists in big rays might prefer 25lb monofilament above the hook because it gives a little better resilience and security if a big fish dives into rocks. Strong nylon also makes a useful handhold should you need to grab a fish from the surf. It is not recommended, but sometimes you have no option.

Hook penetration is always a problem with rays. The jaws are as tough as leather. Timing the strike is never easy and the tendency is to rip trace and bait away before the fish has swallowed the hook. You can avoid missing bites by waiting until the ray moves off with the line. Sometimes it plays with the bait for five minutes before making up its mind. All you can do is sit it out. Keep your hands off the rod, for you can bet that a premature strike will either miss clean or result in a poor hook hold which gives way later.

Long shanked hooks, tough and sharp in

Deep water close to rocks attracts fish after dark. During the day, cast hard for better sport.

*Rays and dogfish must be properly gutted and bled immediately
after capture, otherwise the flesh is discoloured by blood.*

bend and point are mandatory for smalleyed rays. Fine wire, nickel plated 2/0–4/0
Aberdeens are just about satisfactory; the
flimsy blued steel version is useless. Partridge MW hooks are particularly well
tempered and that little thicker in the
wire, so you can use them with confidence. If in doubt scale up to a stronger
pattern like Mustad 79515 and Partridge
Flashpoint. Maintain the point with a file
or slipstone every half dozen casts. Rocks
and even sand dull the point or bend it
over. Either way the hook will skid out of a
smalleyed ray's jaw.

Dogfish

Three species of dogfish haunt the inshore
waters of the British Isles. Lesser spotted
dogs, greater spotted (also called bull
huss) and spurdogs swim close enough inshore to find a beach angler's baits. Most of
the time we try to avoid the lesser spotted
variety which is a pest of plague proportions on some beaches. But huss and spurdogs are nowhere near the menace they
are to boat anglers. In fact a big spurdog
hooked on light tackle in running surf
easily outfights a bass.

77

Most dogfish are located on beaches that fall away to deep water and broken ground. There is a distinct preference for clean water and high salinity. Spurdogs and huss are particularly fussy about their surroundings and even lesser dogs try to stay away from polluted and cloudy water. For these reasons alone dogfish angling is biased towards Atlantic beaches and to cleaner sections of the Channel and upper North Sea.

Habits

Dogfish are hunters and scavengers. Crabs, shrimps, worms and marine life on the sea-bed are all fair game, alive or dead. The bigger species – huss and spurdogs – rip into herrings, sand-eels and mackerel shoals as well as rooting along the sea bottom for anything remotely edible. The good news is that you can use just about any bait. The bad news is that when dogfish really move in, everything else bolts for the horizon.

Beaches are nowhere near as vulnerable to all-out attack as boat marks: though few fishermen choose dogfish as Number One species on the list, there are plenty who would rather hook a dozen doggies than nothing. Match anglers certainly cannot afford to turn up their noses at the thought of a continuous stream of fish weighing between a pound or so (lesser spotted dogs) to upwards of seven pounds for the huss and spurdogs.

Lesser spotted dogfish are residents. They live inshore all year and may thin out only if extremely cold weather forces them to the shelter of deep holes offshore for a few weeks. All sorts of beaches are attractive to this species, though sand, stones and a covering of rocks and weeds are preferred. Unlike the spurdog, lesser spotted dogfish are none too keen on very rough water. Flat conditions and sheltered bays suit them perfectly. They feed at most stages of tide, day and night. Dawn and evening are particularly brisk. The most killing time is on a rising tide which reaches its limit just after dark on a warm autumn night. Big bass, rays and tope creep inshore too, so you might really hit the jackpot.

Tactics and tackle

Ordinary beach tackle is more than a match for lesser spotted dogs. Expect to hook them within 25 yards of the beach, to as far as anyone can cast. Accuracy counts for little on a prime doggy beach – just heave it out there and wait for a bite. Dogs are not too fussy about the kind of bait, or even about its freshness. Big crabs, sand-eels and bunches of ragworm are ideal, but overall fresh, bloody mackerel strips and cross-cut chunks take some beating. Oils and scent attract hunting fish to the hook and trigger a vicious attack. Given its head, a heavy huss or spurdog strips yards of line from the reel.

All dogfish grow sandpaper-like skin and a set of efficient teeth. Lesser dogs are by no means powerful fish but they have a nasty habit of coiling themselves in the

(Opposite) Heavy spurdogs hooked from the surf fight every bit as hard as bass.

The lesser spotted dog is regarded as a pest except for match fishing.

boot. It is kinder than it looks – for both of you.

Spurdogs sometimes invade beaches in vast numbers, although more often they hunt in small packs. Huss are either in small groups or alone. The tendency is for spurdogs to swim along open beaches, while huss lurk in more broken ground often within casting range of a rock platform which gives access to deeper water. Apart from the preferred habitat, the two species have quite a lot in common – from an angling point of view anyway.

Both are strong and potentially quite heavy. Double-figure dogfish are hooked from beaches and rocks, but the main run averages between three and seven pounds. Much depends on where you fish: there are beaches which seldom produce spurdogs over five pounds but as compensation you can catch masses of them. Other marks are more limited in numbers but come up with massive fish now and again. The same pattern emerges with huss.

Summer and autumn bring a lot of good fish all around the coasts, from Scotland to Kent, the West Country, Wales and Ireland. Most are still hooked by accident when you fish for some other species, but as anglers grow to appreciate that dogfish themselves can be a worthwhile challenge from the shore more and more spurdogs and huss fall victim to specialist tactics. Ordinary beach tackle in the 5–6oz bracket is more than adequate for bigger species of dogfish. Hook them one at a time on a running leger or single paternoster rather than on a multi-hook rig; a full house of two or three spurdogs is too much of a handful. Use a strong but sharp hook such as Mustad 79515 Viking or Partridge Flashpoint; 2/0–6/0 is about right, tied to 25–30lb nylon if there are big fish around. On the

trace and literally grinding it apart. Use a 20–25lb snood or trace. If you want to hook them two or three at once, stick to a paternoster; otherwise use a single paternoster or short running leger with a 24in hook link. Be careful of handling a doggy. It will not snap at you, but the skin can scour your hands and arms into a mass of scratches. A two foot lesser dog wrapped around a bare arm can easily draw blood. Wounds are liable to fester unless washed with antiseptic. Instead of grabbing the fish, hold it down with the instep of your whole, a 3/0–4/0 on 20lb line should cope with any dogfish that swims, but you must change the trace every other fish. The nylon soon wears away under a dog's powerful teeth. Very big fish probably merit a short trace of 25–50lb cable-laid stainless steel wire.

9 Surf bass

After a continual pounding by commercial netsmen, the traditional surf beaches of the Atlantic coast are far less productive, but the opportunity to hook bass still exists if you are keen enough to travel. Surf-casting always was hit-and-miss, and never did produce many fish for even the

Heavy winds kick up a vicious surf that may attract bass for only a few hours.

skilled angler. Yet the rewards are great in other respects not least because the true surf beach environment is unique. A 5lb bass, tough and fast from seasons of life in the shifting tides and breakers, outfights a soft-muscled ten pounder hooked from some muddy creek.

'Surf' merits some explanation, for though there are many kinds of rough water along our coastline, only one true surf exists. First, you need the right kind of beach. All surf beaches – also known as storm beaches or in Ireland as strands – are composed of hard-packed sand perhaps interspersed with low rocks. The beach itself slopes so gently that the rising tide pushes between 200 yards and half a mile from the low water mark of spring tides to just short of the high sand dunes which back the foreshore.

The classic surf beach is open and wind-swept, sandwiched between massive headlands that funnel wind and tide. There are vast bays of sand as well, such as Brandon Bay in Eire which is arguably the biggest beach in Europe. Closer to home, the major bays of Cornwall and Wales offer plenty of space for surf to generate. Two kinds of surf action are involved: local surf and swell surf.

Surf action

Local winds and direct tidal action roughen the water from a ripple to a full-blooded sea with high rollers and tables of white surf. This local pattern is always accompanied by a stiff wind. The water is dirty, sometimes so filled with weed that within a minute of casting out you are fighting a mass of vegetation which threatens to break your line. Fishing can be excellent but usually tails off during the height of the storm and improves as it dies away.

The keen bass man prefers real swell surf, perhaps with only a gentle breeze blowing onshore to maintain the action.

Indeed, genuine swell surf roars on to the sand even when there is no wind. Sometimes a massive force of water drives ashore into the teeth of an offshore gale; you cast a mile, yet the waves literally push you back up the sand. The swells are created by storms far out in the ocean. The water is stirred violently and the swells radiate like ripples around a stone dropped into calm water. The humps of moving water drive over the continental shelf, slide towards the coast then dump their

Swell surf produces the steady tables of water and waves which hold bass for long periods.

Sand-eel rigged on a short snood paternoster.

Bare sand and rushing water disguise the teeming marine life which lives on a surf beach. Sand is a gentle medium with plenty of space, oxygen and water for small animals. At the lowest limits of the tideline live razor fish, clams and lugworms. Even in the wildest surf, sand-eels and crabs exist happily under the sand's protection. Small fish, plankton and fry inhabit the water itself. The surf beach throbs with life.

Calm water on rising or falling tides encourages the marine creatures to hide. They are keyed up to the dangers of clear water, bright sunlight and marauding predators – bigger fish, sea-birds and their own kind. During the day, species like bass, rays and tope tend to remain lingering far beyond casting range in deeper, darker water where they themselves feel safe. Surf action triggers a change in mood, especially with bass which are tolerant of swirling water and suspended sand. Swells rip up the sand, rake out food and wash it into the plateaux of water between the breakers. Then the bass move in.

Habits

Bass show a two-way movement according to conditions, time and tide. Calm, clear weather sends them offshore; surf encourages them in. While they are inshore they patrol sections of beach, feeding here, skipping several hundred yards of sand, settling elsewhere to feed again. If the surf remains constant – which it will do only in swell surf conditions on exposed beaches – the cycle is repeated with each tide. Catch a bass one hour after low water, and you can be fairly confident of hooking another fish from the same shoal or group at the same stage of the next tide. This rhythm of

energy on to the shoreline as heavy surf.

The fetch of the waves – that is, the distance they travel over the open seas – is an important factor. It takes time and space to build a significant swell action which arrives on the beach as day or week-long pounding surf rather than a few hours of lightweight action. The sheer logistics of the exercise rule out good swell surf fishing in Britain except on the Atlantic coast. You may find a short, sometimes vicious surf on east coast bass beaches, but never the high, lazy swells which roll in day after day from the westerly ocean.

These days a five pound bass from the surf is a specimen.

fishing probably holds the secrets of catching surf bass.

The bigger tides and changeable weather of spring and autumn equinox tides are always a hot time for surf bass, as they are for all kinds of sea fish everywhere. There is a link between big tides and winds; you may have noticed that the wind blows harder in late April and early October. On the exposed western beaches the effects are especially pronounced. Sometimes beaches are hit by storms that make fishing impossible. Or the winds themselves remain at sea but fuel day after day

of prime surf conditions. Keen to fatten for the lean winter ahead, autumn bass feed strongly and will hit your baits harder than at any other time of year.

Baits

Sheltered surf beaches and the backwaters and estuaries often associated with true storm beaches are a natural breeding ground for lugworms. For years, bass fishermen forked up boxes of big worms to bait their hooks. They work well: tough for casting, juicy and easily visible against a

85

backdrop of sand. Of all the baits used to catch bass from the open surf, lugworms headed the list because of their availability and apparent superiority. Many surf anglers well versed in tides and the habits of their fish never bothered to look at alternatives.

Razor fish and clams are worth considering as well. Clams are the big, soft-shelled bivalves found when you dig lugworms in fairly clean sand or sand with a little mud. The long siphon that protrudes from the shell when the animal lies buried makes an extremely tough bass bait by itself, and combines with a bunch of lugworms to make a hookful no fish can resist.

To dig clams specifically, look for a neat hole drilled into the sand near a damp but not waterlogged section of the lower beach. The tell-tale sign is a jet of water squirted up to a foot into the air; it is more powerful and noticeable than the brief jet thrown up by big ragworms. Drive the fork tines full length into the sand so that the hole is neatly in the centre of the spit, and keep digging. Most anglers miss them be-

The bass of a lifetime – 13½lb from the surf on squid bait.

cause they give up the search too soon. Some anglers prefer to wash the shells and store the bivalve in a bucket of sea water. Others reckon bait lasts longer if the dirty shells are packed into a damp box. Crack the shell, tear out the entire siphon for bait, and save the innards in case you run out of siphons.

Once virtually a secret bait, sand-eels are now used for all kinds of beach fishing. Rock and beach fishermen in Cornwall are especially adept at sand-eel fishing; in their view it is the finest bait for virtually all their fishing. Certainly for bass there is nothing finer. Anglers elsewhere might not go all the way with the Cornish view, but at least they agree that the sand-eel has a great deal to offer if only as part of a more versatile bait armoury. Their role in surf bass fishing is immense though, and no keen bass man can afford to pass up any chance of at least trying them.

Sand-eels are easily caught by raking or netting. Netting is quicker and more productive, but an hour's raking along the tideline is worth a fortune if the bass are preoccupied with sand-eels, as they often are in autumn and spring. The bait has saved the day for anglers who found themselves beaten by shoals of bass that ignored the usual worms and clams. The best sand-eel is a live one, so consider investing in an aerated cooler box for your travels. If you are bassing nearer home, tank the sand-eels for long-term storage and take them fishing in an ice pack.

Squid and fish baits are normally thought of as an outside bet. Sometimes they work extremely well, but hardly ever in terms of numbers. The surf bass hooked on a side of mackerel or whole squid is likely to be a monster. But the odds are that you will never see a fish like that; on

Light rods casting 4oz of lead are the right blend of power and control for surf work.

most surf beaches, squid and mackerel are baits for the dedicated big-fish man who is prepared to spend days or months chasing one specimen fish.

The beauty of mackerel – squid is borderline here – is its universal appeal to rays, tope, spurdogs, conger, pollack and the other species which may also be around. All of them, conger included, will move into the fringes of the surf at night. Very long casting sometimes picks up species which the old-time anglers never dreamt of hooking from the open surf. The value of a mackerel bait, and perhaps squid, is that you automatically cover another side of the sport at the same time as you fish for the bass. With bass stocks falling it makes sense to have an option. If necessary, fish with two rods: one with mackerel, the other hand-held and baited with a 'proper' bass bait like worms.

King ragworms are usually an excellent bait. On eastern bass grounds and along the south coasts, you can do no better than thread a chunk of bloody, lively ragworm on to your bass rig. The situation is different in the storm beach environment. Though one hesitates to lay down rules here, experience strongly points to one conclusion: on the majority of open surf beaches when the surf is running properly, ragworm makes a very poor bait for anything except flounders.

Some Welsh and Cornish beaches fall midway between true surf strands and ordinary sandbanks, and in estuaries particularly ragworm is a killer for bass and the general fish population. King ragworm works beautifully, closely followed by harbour ragworms and whites. Matchmen might prefer the smaller worms because they tend to excel with flatties and eels, the two major species essential for making up weights. Few matches are won with bass.

Tactics and tackle

Presentation counts more in the surf than in average beach fishing. You may fish for a week with an ordinary paternoster and catch bass after bass, day and night. Then the fish stop biting. You know they are still there but whereas last night they hit your bait, tonight they ignore it. Change baits – no response; but switch to a running leger

and you are back in action. Even an extended snood might do the trick.

Short snoods are better in rough water, longer ones in calm. The 9–12 inch snooded paternoster used in whiting and flatty fishing works well but you will probably prefer to cast one bait instead of the usual two or three. When the surf dies down extend the snood to 24 inches; if that tangles switch to the running paternoster, a most popular surf rig which offers tangle-free fishing, good presentation and yet still casts a long way. Use bait clips if you want those extra yards.

Just as important as the exact rig format – and I think perhaps more important in some ways – are the hooks. Bass in surf must surely be conditioned into picking up food that is washed around by the swells or is actively swimming around in the shallow, swirling water. A bait so heavily weighted by sinker and hook that it sinks and just lies inert could be a turn-off. Test lightweight hooks like Aberdeens and Spearpoints if you cannot get good results on the normal brands; sometimes they make a vast difference.

Five to six ounce beach tackle fished from a rod rest planted on dry sand takes its toll of surf bass. When bass run the beaches, feeding hard on sand-eels and worms, there is no need to cast very far or to feel for the tiniest bite. A rested rod signals the bite and gives plenty of time to reel in hooked fish. Something is missing though: to fish that way is completely divorced, mentally and physically, from the inner world of the surf beach. Throw away your rod rest and tackle box, pull on a pair of long boots and wade out there with just rod and bait.

Half an hour fishing with a normal beachcaster strains your arms and your

Ordinary beach rods are a better bet if heavy fish must be lifted out bodily.

or two ounces, with a proportionate step down in line test from 12–15lb to 8–10lb. The snag is that you might well lose bass or hook them in the stomach because the inertia of smaller leads is insufficient to drive home the hook. At least 3oz rigged with grip wires, or 4–5oz of plain lead, are necessary to set a trap for feeding bass. In the long run anglers who fish slightly heavy catch more bass, especially when fish hit shy and short.

Modern glass fibre and semi-carbon rods about 11½ feet long, balanced to cast 4oz perfectly yet able to handle 5oz at a push, are light and easy to hold all day. The finest blanks weigh less than 10oz. Made up with lined rings, FPS seat and rubber grips (much superior to cork in these saturated conditions) the rod need not exceed 16oz. The easy action blends 100 yard-plus fishing with soft baits to the essential option of lobbing just 20 yards if necessary. It is surprisingly difficult to control short casts on a stiff rod when accuracy also is at stake.

Wide open surf beaches encourage you to fish by yourself. Then you can safely afford to reduce leader breaking strain. Twenty to thirty pound high-grade monofilament holds a 4oz cast together and enhances bait action. Sometimes thick leaders deter bass from taking the bait; over-stiff traces also reduce bites. Bass are by no means cunning or fussy as a rule, but where you can afford to cut line diameter without losing control, do it.

Bites and landing

The mechanics of surf bassing are secondary to picking the right time and presenting good baits. Bass respond to any form of legering, either paternoster or running

patience. Water pours ashore in rolling swells, but no sideways current tears line and sinker along the beach. Even a 2oz sinker holds nicely. What about a lighter rod? Fishermen who spend days and nights in the surf casting to bass running 25 to 150 yards from the shallows, insist on light, well balanced rods. They do not compromise on reels either – it is multipliers only. Fixed spools never seem to blend with a surf rod, destroying smooth, fast handling of bites and hooked fish.

Sometimes you can afford to drop to one

trace. Bait the hook heavily and work the surf line from twenty yards beyond comfortable wading depth to maximum range. The old theory about bass hunting the third breaker is surprisingly accurate; the wave coincides with a nice depth of water, strong undertow combing food from inshore sand and easy casting range with soft baits. Eighty yards is about right on the majority of beaches. Cast out, tighten up on the sinker and feel for bites with finger and thumb looped on the line. Strike anything that moves.

Slack line or rod-bending bites happen any time. Mostly, bass pick up the hook and run. A double-tug followed by a steady run is characteristic of bold surf bass. They can also suck in a bait without shifting the sinker an inch. Be ready for a tough fight; no risk of being smashed if you take your time but exhilarating for all that. Keep the rod tip high, set the clutch to medium tension and apply extra pressure on the spool with your thumb.

Never force the issue when the bass rolls into the last line of breaking surf where swells and backwash can pick up a ten pounder and either swill it high up the beach (the object of the exercise) or sweep it out to sea so quickly that the line snaps. Lift the fish on to a wave and let the sea do the beaching. Guide the fish ashore and grab it. Avoid dorsal spines and sharp gill plates.

(Opposite) Hold a bass by the lower jaw to avoid the sharp gill plates and dorsal fin spikes.

10 Congers and smoothhounds

Conger eel

A tough conger eel threatening to pull you and the rod down the rocks is the ultimate experience in shorefishing or a nightmare, depending on how you respond to the challenge. For every angler in love with conger eel fishing there are a hundred scared stiff of the very idea of latching on to a big one. Congers bulge with muscle and they live in dense cover. In common with all big predators they sit tight for hours on end, then attack. Consequently, catching an eel is something of a hit and miss exercise unless you study form: baits, casting range, tidal cycle and season. The most successful conger anglers pick their time and place after a great deal of spadework. Even then few big congers are hooked in relation to the hours spent fishing.

A conger eel is potentially among the biggest fishes in North Atlantic seas. Boat-caught eels in the 75lb-plus bracket are relatively common, whereas shore-caught conger over 50lb are reported only once or twice a season. Why the disparity? Few shore anglers specialise in eels; and even if you hook a monster the chances of landing

it are slim. Boat men have the advantage of direct lift which hauls the eel into clear water.

Congers are not confined to deep water and they do not mind being temporarily exposed by low spring tides. Winkling out stranded congers from kelp and rocks is a favourite pastime in the Channel Islands where rise and fall of tides is far more pronounced than on the mainland. Anglers wander along the low tide line to gaff eels from pools and crevices. On the whole though, deepish water with rocks and weeds that are always covered at low tide prove better congering grounds than more gently sloping beaches. If you cast into at least fifteen feet of water on the low tide, conger fishing is likely to prove more predictable and to offer a far higher number of eels weighing more than twenty pounds.

The exception is where surplus food is available. If a conger does not have to hunt fast-moving fishes and crustaceans it saves energy and grows faster. Free dinners according to the conger's shopping list include fish offal and garbage, both associated with harbours and piers. Wherever

(Opposite) A fifteen pound conger eel from the harbour wall at St Catherine's, Jersey.

trawlers dump fish guts overboard and waste falls into the sea through drainpipes or is thrown over pier rails and harbour walls, eels move in to feed on rubbish and small fish which congregate naturally.

Open-sea eels feed better at dusk and on through the night. Tide matters little as long as the hunting ground remains covered. These 'wild' congers are fond of wandering on to clean sand, well away from the normal rocky lair. Harbour congers sometimes venture into the open but are instinctively cautious and always nervous about leaving themselves vulnerable.

But they do learn to slot into the pattern of the man-made environment. Rather than feed strictly to tide and time patterns they lie in wait until fish gutting and net cleaning begin. Then virtually regardless of daylight and water clarity they sneak out to feed. But they seldom make the mistake of straying far from a crevice in the rocks.

Eels in their natural habitat shun semi-rotten fish baits, and in extreme circumstances ignore a bait unless it is alive. Small pollack and coalfish, pouting and baby mackerel, even big crabs and sand-eels are necessary to induce a bite. Harbour fish

Congers are not afraid of man. Probably the majority of eels live alongside harbours, jetties and breakwaters.

are accustomed to easier pickings and do take stale fish baits. A chunk of soft, greasy mackerel works wonders. The important consideration is to give them the food they prefer; and that comes back to knowing your particular group of eels and their habits.

Baits and traces

Good bait makes the difference between hauling out a stream of quality congers or sitting behind the rod for days and nights on end without a bite. If you opt to fish for harbour conger, start with some kind of fish bait, the oilier and bloodier the better. Herrings, mackerel and assorted fish guts (livers are excellent) make fine openers. For 'wild' congers, try absolutely fresh mackerel fillets, fish-frozen squid and big sand-eels, live and dead. Baits can be fairly small because despite their great weight and healthy appetites conger eels are surprisingly slow, cautious feeders.

Response to a smallish bait is positive, while an over-generous helping leads to delay and missed bites. Congers must be hit hard and clean. Skidding hooks muffled by layers of soft bait lose eel after eel, and the denser the cover the more critical striking becomes. The trouble with conger eels is that they fight backwards. Every other species of fish we hook from the beach either lies doggo relying on its body weight for protection, or swims off head first. Congers are adept at shuffling backwards while spinning and thrashing like demons. The tail probes the sea-bed for anything solid for the eel to grip or wriggle into. Once anchored even a small conger grits its teeth and holds steady until bodily torn away from its hiding place.

Crimp a 4–6/0 Seamaster or O'Shaugh-

nessy, well honed to a chisel point, to 18 inches of 100lb cable-laid wire or 80–130lb monofilament. Fix the upper end of the trace to a strong swivel and tie that into a running leger rig with a 3–6oz sinker sliding freely on the shock leader. Bait the hook with a chunk of mackerel or squid and be sure hook point and barb stand bare. Cast into the rough ground, set the reel in free spool, ratchet clicked on, and wait for a conger to steal the bait.

Feel for the bite – a crafty conger takes line against the ratchet inch by inch.

Night conger fishing

As darkness falls, check that your gaff is to hand and that you know the safest route down to the water's edge. Fish with other anglers working as a team: one on the rod, one at the gaff, the third holding the lamp. Just sit it out until fish show up. Replace baits every twenty minutes.

The sea washes against the base of the rocks and the pressure of swells bounces the rod tip in a regular beat. Keep your eyes glued to the tip ring. For all their size and power conger eels bite gently. The bigger they are the less you may see. Watch for a changing pattern that sets the tip bouncing as smoothly as before but out of step with the swells. Two or three inches of line click from the reel and run out from the tip ring into the darkness. Keep your hands off the rod. Give the eel time to creep away with the bait. The tackle lies on clean sand less than ten yards from the rocks, so there is a bit of leeway. Another foot of line disappears up the rings. The eel is heading for home, reaching backwards with that powerful tail towards the safety of weeds and stones.

Prod the hook free with a disgorger or forceps. Deeply hooked fish should have the trace snipped short.

Pick up the rod, push the reel into gear and switch off the ratchet. Point the rod directly at the fish and take up slack line. Feel the conger's weight, then lift as hard and as high as possible. Pull the hook home and crank the eel off the sea-bed. That drumming pressure on the line is the eel desperately backing away, spinning the trace as she probes for a tailhold.

Whatever happens, keep that line tight. Heavy tackle is a great asset for congering; a powerful beach blank rigged to 25lb line or even stronger if you aim to haul a big eel out of atrocious ground offers a little extra winching power. Baby surf rods and tiny reels have no place in this sport. Despite what the exponents of light surfcasting suggest, congering is a rugged sport, definitely not for flimsy tackle and delicate technique.

Either you pull hard enough to lift the eel away from the obstructions, or she retaliates by wrapping herself and your trace so firmly in the rocks that pulling all night long would not break the grip. A conger prefers to die rather than admit defeat. So get that rod working: lift and pump until the line sings with tension.

Your conger skids against a rock ledge, momentarily snags then breaks free. You can feel her rubbery body writhe and spin through the weeds. Congers hardly run in the accepted sense but you cannot afford to take chances with the drag setting. Never overtighten the star wheel when the eel is on the surface, lashing towards the shore.

Stand still while the others see to the gaffing. The height of your rock platform puts you right over the fish – the most practical and most effective place to be. At the last moment, slacken off and control the spool with thumb pressure. Hold the eel on the surface while waves wash her closer to the gaff.

They've missed her . . . it happens all the time with congers. They are notoriously hard to gaff. Let her go down a few feet then pump her back to the top. This time the gaff goes in. The eel spins wildly on the gaff shaft as they drag her up the rocks to safe ground. According to the cynics, the real fight begins now. Congers thrash around uncontrollably, but they are not dangerous if you keep clear of jaws and tail. Besides, this is a small fish, not more than twenty pounds. The hook is deep inside her throat so dispense with a disgorger. Cut the trace close to the lips then push her back into the water.

I assume you would rather put the eel back. Some anglers kill conger eels because they are scared stiff. Very few eat them although the meat from a young fish is reasonably good. Skinned and cut into chunks, conger eel bakes and steams well enough but the strong flavour is not to everyone's taste. Conservation is unnecessary in sheer survival terms; there are millions of congers in the sea. But why kill a fish just for the sake of it? Congers suffer more torture and bad handling than any other species except sharks, and all because of their undeserved notoriety for savagery and snake-like cunning.

Smoothhounds

Modern smoothhound fishing began some ten years ago. I recall reading little about the species before that although the occasional fish was hooked by boat and beach men, usually by accident. Then Essex charter boats and beach fishermen began to pick them up in big numbers from the Blackwater estuary and offshore marks. Suddenly smoothhound fishing was the latest craze. As more fishermen homed in on the species hotspots established themselves around the British coasts. Smoothhounds had been there all the time but nobody had bothered to fish for them.

I caught my first smoothhound from a dinghy anchored at the mouth of a tiny inland creek of the Blackwater, almost at its saltwater limits. We had landed a few bass and eels during the flood tide, top water and early ebb but now the fish were gone and crabs tore the ragworm bait to shreds. I lifted the rod to change baits, wound the tackle a few inches off the bottom then the rod banged down on the gunwales as something big and fast grabbed the hook and made off downstream. My 20lb line snapped like cotton because I had forgotten to set the clutch.

We were nearly out of bait, and soon the dropping tide would force us back to the main estuary channel. As a last ditch stand I retackled and hooked on a small hardbacked crab which lay cowering in the bilges. Within five minutes of hitting the sea-bed, the tackle screamed off downtide again. This time I checked the drag tension before striking.

The fish battled for ten minutes before coming aboard. It looked like a tope, weighed 25lb and thrashed wildly on the bottom boards. But something was wrong: tope are not so dumpy as that. The dorsal fin looked wrong as well, and above all this fish lacked the sharp, cutting teeth of the tope family. Its teeth were flat and interlocked like paving slabs, almost identical to those of a thornback ray.

Bigger than a spurdog, lacking a dorsal spine and clumsier than a tope, the smoothhound is quite easy to identify. The simplest distinction between tope and smoothhounds is dentition, which can always be relied upon as *the* tell-tale sign. It is more difficult to differentiate between starry and common species of smoothhounds. The common is a little bigger and usually lacks spots. But some commons do have spots; while some starry fish are plain. Identification is a scientific process which takes into account tooth structure and other slight anatomical variations. Should you hook a potential record, have it identified by a marine biologist or museum.

Habits

Smoothhounds arrive inshore in summer. Boat anglers crop the shoals some weeks before they drift into casting range of beaches and creeks. Sometimes the beach invasion is as late as September, but more often you should pick them up by late July.

August and early September are the peak time for numbers caught and highest average size. Fishing is a clear cut on-off procedure: expect either to draw a blank or to hook a stream of fish.

The smoothhound is said to be a scavenger and predator. Of all the prey available to it, above all the fish loves common shore crabs and hermits. It matters not whether they are hard shelled or soft; unlike the majority of shoreline species, hounds readily accept a hardback green crab from the hook. As a temporary measure when you cannot find a supply of crabs, try king ragworm or whole baby squid.

I am far from convinced about the smoothhound's scavenging habits. Most are crammed with crabs and small fish. Yet they are a species that delights in rooting through the sea-bed where garbage and fish offal is thrown overboard from yachts and commercial fishing craft. The explanation goes beyond mere scavenging: rather than attack the mess itself, smoothhounds go for an easy kill on the crabs which are preoccupied with their own feeding. Certainly, when the crab hordes thin out in late autumn, the smoothhounds are long gone.

Feeding patterns

Creek and open beach smoothhounds work to a tidal feeding pattern which varies with season and place, influenced by weather and light intensity. Essex

(Opposite) A hard-fighting inshore smoothhound of fifteen pounds. This is a common smoothhound, Mustelus mustelus.

smoothhounds feed better on the early flood rather than at high tide. Sport is better in overcast weather but for some reason night fishing from the shore is never as good as in half-light at dawn or dusk.

Unlike whiting and flat-fish that feed throughout the tidal cycle, hounds are far more choosy. During any twenty-four hour period they might feed within casting range for no more than thirty minutes. They do not lay up in one spot to feed; the pattern is one of continuous movement as fish hunt along a predetermined pathway, feeding to a timetable against which you can set your watch. If the mouth of a creek

produces smoothhounds one hour after low water on Tuesday morning, they will be back at the same stage of flood on Wednesday, Thursday or until their habits change naturally or are disrupted by weather or excessive boat traffic.

For tidal reasons the feeding time of smoothhound shoals that invade estuary creeks is later than at the river mouth itself. In those permanently covered channels fish feed as soon as the tide makes. Start fishing at low water and follow the shoal upstream as the flood forces water upriver. If you cannot stay in contact, switch marks progressively. Look for natu-

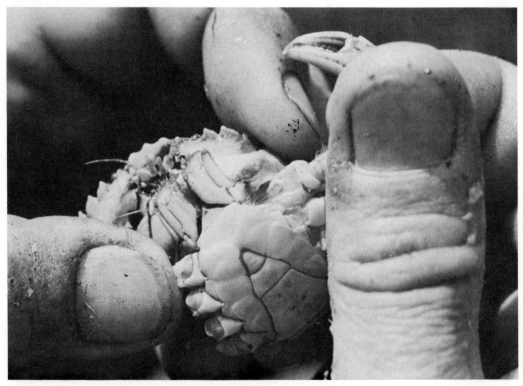

Whole or legless peeler crab is the supreme smoothhound bait.

Packs of fish sometimes hunt close inshore along sandy and gravel beaches in the east and south-east.

ral hotspots where the main channel branches into side creeks and tributaries.

Time and water depth help pinpoint the best fishing time. Aim to start fishing at dead low water. On neaps, go by the water depth: smoothhounds are reluctant to venture into too-shallow water, and they never risk being stranded by the ebb. On the whole it is advisable to fish in at least four feet of water. Six to fifteen feet is even better, especially in bright conditions. An Admiralty chart holds valuable information on water depth in your local area and saves months of survey work on the shore.

A classic mark

Bradwell Creek at the mouth of the Blackwater is a fine smoothhound mark. Tucked into the south bank of the river some two miles from the open sea, the creek shrinks back to a fifty yard channel at low tide, three to five feet deep and flanked by mudflats, weeds and shell-grit. On a still, hot evening in late September water rises in the creek and bubbles over the mud-flats. The creek broadens and deepens as the tide pushes in from the sea. Yachts moored in the creek lift from the mud and swing their

101

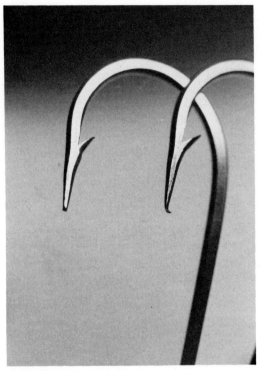

Hone the hook to a chisel point (left).
A long needle point (right) kinks
against the hound's tough jaws.

bows into the current. That is a signal to
start fishing. Bait with a two to three inch
peeler crab or a big hermit and cast into
the middle of the channel.

Four to five ounce plain sinkers hold
bottom in the young flood. Later in the
tide grip wires are necessary but at first it
does not matter if the tackle does drift
along the creek bed; it may even help
locate the fish. An ordinary running paternoster presents the bait on a two to three
foot trace of 30lb monofilament. A tough
leader buffers the cast and resists the

hound's sandpaper skin. Apart from that,
tackle is absolutely standard beach fishing
gear.

Tackle and tactics

With thousands of crabs homing in on the
bait immediately it hits the mud, you must
rebait every ten minutes at most. Even
squid are mashed to pulp in a quarter of an
hour. Keep baiting and casting, and after
every cast throw the reel out of gear and
set the ratchet. Preset the drag as well – a
big fish never gives you a second chance.
Some fish mouth the bait, others tug, most
take a couple of preliminary pulls. Whatever the case there follows a rapid and
powerful run, sometimes seawards, sometimes up-creek. Let the fish go. Hit a
smoothhound in the first five yards and
you will almost certainly miss. Fifteen
yards of line stream off the reel before the
experienced smoothhound angler throws
the gear lever, thumbs the spool and drives
in the hook. It is like hitting a brick wall;
this is one species of saltwater fish that
never gives up the ghost at the first touch
of steel.

Smoothhounds run so hard that there is
no chance to stop them dead. Even 30lb
line makes no impression on a 20lb fish
heading upriver in top gear. What they
may lack in speed is counterbalanced by
power and determination. Let her run out
of steam (most are females) then tighten
the clutch and pump line back on to the
reel. Expect second, third and fourth runs
shorter than the first but still strong and
unstoppable.

Gaffing is unnecessary. Hounds lash in
all directions, squirm like snakes and tie
tackle in knots but they are not in the least
dangerous. The tough skin provides a per-

fect handgrip, so grab the fish by the tail root and lift it ashore. Treat the fish gently: strong and heavy, robust and lively a smoothhound may be, yet it cannot stand rough handling. Like all the cartilaginous species it relies on water pressure to support its internal organs. Lifting alone may rupture the major blood sinuses. Pick it up by the tail and support the head with your other hand. Lay the fish on the beach, snip off the trace or flip out the hook with pliers, then slide it back into the sea.

11 Wrasse, pouting and silver eels

Wrasse

From the tropics to the poles, from Atlantic to Pacific, wherever the shoreline drops quickly into deep, rocky water there are brightly coloured fish that live in the deepest crevices and weed beds. Adapted for life close to the rock faces, they eat shellfish, crustaceans and small fish. Some are big, hard fighting species with a sporting pedigree, but mostly they are small, plentiful and easy to hook. In Britain it is the wrasse that fills this ecological slot. Most North Atlantic species are of little value in angling: goldsinny, rock cook, cuckoo, corkwing and rainbow wrasse are either too small to bother with or so unusual that they are caught purely by chance. The wrasse for shore fishing is the ballan, *Labrus bergylta*.

A wrasse is almost impossible to confuse with any of the common saltwater fish. The ballan looks very much like a highly coloured sea-going carp. It is a slab-sided fish, powerful but compact whose shape does not hint at speed. It is built to withstand buffeting in swells that drive into the rocks. The big scales are camouflaged in greens and browns with flashes of orange, red and purple which blend with shadowy weeds and boulders. Teeth are small, square and evenly placed inside rubbery lips, perfect weapons to crunch crabs and chisel barnacles.

Wrasse are a deep water species found in 20–100ft with a preference for clean, well oxygenated water and dense cover. Virtually all serious wrasse fishing takes place from the rocks of the West Country, Wales, Ireland and Scotland. Occasional wrasse are hooked from shallowish beaches but as a rule you must fish from the open sea cliffs and breakwaters for specimens. Small fish find their way into harbours and under piers.

The average ballan wrasse weighs under 3lb, but 3–5lb fish are common enough, especially if you fish legered baits, and even bigger fish are there for the taking. According to fishermen hunting bass, tope and conger in very broken ground, the wrasse record could be smashed any time by a good angler who bothered to go after them. The wrasse, you see, is one of fishing's second-class citizens.

In days of flat calm where surf beaches lie asleep and bassless, and nothing much stirs from the rocks either, good old wrasse can be relied upon to inject some life into the sport. On the right tackle they really do fight well, not least because they are so adept at wrapping line and trace around the nearest chunk of granite. Every wrasse owns a set of bolt-holes as complex as a rabbit warren.

Divers and fisheries biologists report

Shoals of wrasse live alongside the rock faces in deep, turbulent water.

that wrasse in their natural environment lurk very close to the rock faces, lying with their tails backed into chinks and holes. They sneak behind weed clumps and tuck themselves into the sand at the base of the rock walls. Some cruise a few yards from cover, but generally wrasse stay close to home. The lessons for anglers are clear enough: fish in the rough stuff and cast short. Much depends on the lie of the land of course. If the rock platform you fish from drops sheer to clean sand, the baits go in right under your feet. Elsewhere it may be necessary to cast out to an inshore reef.

Either way, aim to drop the bait on to the rocks or very close against the base, even though this means losing tackle.

Tactics

For years floatfishing was the accepted wrassing technique. A short trace hanging two feet under a ½–2oz drilled bullet buoyed by a sliding float drifts the bait along the margins of the rocks. This way you gain a fair amount of control and reduce tackle losses. More important, variations in bait depth and float path

105

help you to search the entire mark.

Average wrasse do not mind attacking a big hook loaded with bait. There is no reason to pursue that theme though. A small, very sharp hook well tempered and short shanked is far easier to sink into the fish's leathery jaws, and smaller baits encourage clean hooking. Big baits and oversize hooks force the wrasse to attack with its teeth rather than by simply swallowing. Point and barb either miss or skid from the incisors.

Limpets, sand-eel chunks and some-times worms are the favourite wrasse baits. Try a 4–6 carp hook tied to 12–15lb nylon which resists teeth and abrasive rocks. Leave the hook point standing proud of the bait. Start by plumbing water depth, then set the float to carry baits just off the bottom. Trot the float down the shoreline, starting close in to the rocks and working out a yard or two at a time. Then raise the baits a foot and try again. Wrasse seem to stratify at specific depths, as do pollack and other rock species.

The ballan wrasse.

Pouting

Pouting are the scrapings of sea angling's barrel or one of the most important fish in the sea, depending on whether you go match fishing. They are small fish weighing a couple of pounds at best, do not fight and taste like nothing on earth. He is a desperate man who keeps pouting for the pot. Related to cod and whiting they share a preference for cool water and bottom-feeding. Most pouting stay well offshore throughout the year, resident on wrecks and over broken ground. Smaller fish move inshore onward of late autumn but they still prefer deepish water over their backs.

You are more likely to hook pouting from steeply shelving beaches and rock marks than from estuary flats and surf beaches. However, very long casts over shallow ground may find a shoal of pouting willing to feed. They offer a bonus to expert casters fishing a match on an otherwise barren strip of sea-bed. A handful of pouting may be enough to scoop the prizes in a competition that has everyone scratching desperately for a few fish.

Out in deep water, pouting live in semi-darkness at best. When they migrate inshore they never lose a basic fear of sunshine and bright surroundings. During the day they lie up under cover and hardly touch a bait unless it lands right on their nose. Sometimes they ignore food altogether. As soon as the sun drops low enough though, pouting wake up. Then the sea is alive with tiny fish seldom weighing more than a pound, which snatch baits from the hook as fast as you can rebait and throw out. Two and three hook paternosters are hauled ashore with a pouting on every snood. Serious bass, whiting and cod anglers regard them as a

Strong teeth used to chisel shellfish from rock faces.

plague worse than dogfish.

Match anglers make the most of it. Five to fifteen pounds of pouting sets a tough pace for the rest of the field. You face very long odds in the same contest by persisting with big baits and hooks aimed at, say, cod. On most beaches these days, salvation in the form of a 20lb cod rarely happens. As a result top match anglers never miss an opportunity to slam into the pouting shoals.

107

Baits and tackle

Pouting are content to eat anything. Lugworms, ragworms, fish strips, crabs, sandeels and squid are favoured hook baits. In deep, clean water pouting sometimes snatch artificial lures and spinners cast for pollack and codling, but few anglers spin deliberately for them.

Bait selection is governed by whether you want to catch or avoid them. Matchmen use the very best and most attractive baits simply because pouting are too im-portant to miss. Sporting qualities – which amount to very little – never enter the argument. Worms, crabs, and fish strips all encourage a rapid attack. The sooner a pouting shoal rips a hundred worms to bits, the better; by then the bag should be mounting up.

Anglers fishing for cod, bass or any of the 'proper' beach species adopt special tactics to avoid their baits being chewed by over-enthusiastic pouting. Worms and crabs are taboo when pouting are feeding flat out; no matter how much you load on, even a

The pouting (below) is often confused with the more slender whiting.

skinny pout will eventually grind its way through the food and on to the hook point. Very much tougher baits are essential. Try whole squid, mackerel fillet and live sand-eels; at least that way you delay the inevitable long enough for a real fish to come along. The odds are poor even so. It often seems that other species stay away while pouting are on a spree. The best you can hope for is a pack of tope or spurdogs to thin out the pests.

Tactics

Paternosters are the best rig. Three hook rigs boost catch rate and short snoods counteract the pouting's trick of knitting itself into a web of nylon. Snoods should be of reasonably thick nylon about 15–20lb test because one by one the fish you hook slowly grind away the line just above the hook. After a hectic hour's pout bashing the snood is severely weakened. It does not matter much if you lose a pouting, but the next fish might just be a cod or pan-sized flatty.

Small hooks are by no means essential. Small pouting happily gorge a 2/0 hook, so on that score it makes little difference what you use. However, hooks tend to go down a long way. Disgorgers and long-nosed forceps are sometimes useless because you cannot see the hook trapped deep in the fish's belly. Here the fine wire blue Aberdeen hook comes into its own: hold the fish down and jerk the trace free.

Concerned matchmen try to keep pouting alive for weighing-in. They are not the toughest survivors but should last for a couple of hours in a bucket of sea water. Unfortunately, the species cannot easily accommodate a rapid change in pressure, so hauling them from thirty feet of water is enough to swell and perhaps even rupture the swim bladder. Of all the fish in the sea, pouting suffer most at the hands of anglers. Even careful handling is potentially lethal.

Silver eels

Too many beach fishermen think that eels are so easy to catch that you never need to worry about tackle and baits. Bootlace eels certainly do fall into the suicidal category and will hit any old bait presented on the crudest rig. But for real success and to pick up the specimens, top eel men are very fussy about their tackle. The tactics used by Thames experts is an object lesson in forward planning and precise execution.

Rods, reels and lines are second string to some extent, chosen with general beach fishing in mind. Casting power, action, length of rod, choice of multiplier or fixed spool reel, sinker weight and line test are largely matters of personal preference. In those departments eel tackle is no different than any other. However it is fun to hook them on light tackle where tide and distance allow; hard though they fight, eels are relatively small-time in the sea league and there is no point cranking them out on super-heavy gear if a change to light surf or even carp tackle makes life more interesting.

Terminal rigs

Terminal rigs have a tremendous bearing on success with shore eels. Ordinary short-snood paternosters as used by thousands of keen beach men do not produce many eels. If you were to fish the prolific Thames eel

Pouting sometimes become a real pest in late afternoon, robbing the hook as soon as you cast.

marks with a traditional paternoster using hooks supported by standard 6–9in snoods, the locals would thrash you ten fish to one. When eels are fussy about feeding, ordinary rigs fail to attract a single bite no matter what the bait. It is hard to believe that the right rig and a wrong one fished side by side and baited identically should be so different. In this sense eels are a challenge indeed, far more choosy than species that are reckoned to know a thing or two about terminal gear.

The secret is to extend the paternoster snoods to at least 18in. The extra 6–9in

of nylon between stand-off and hook really do revolutionise your eel fishing. Tie your new rig in the normal manner using regular stand-off loops, Avis booms or bead-trapped swivels depending on your preference. Forget tales you might hear about eel rigs having to be made tangle-free; avoidance of knitting depends more on how you handle the eel than on any particular rig design.

Snood breaking strain of 10–15lb proves satisfactory for routine eeling, though if you must cast hard wind knots may form too easily in the lighter tests. Bait clips are one answer. Hooks? Fine wire and medium shank are the telling features. Seamatch Eyed are popular and regular eyed Aberdeens will do at a pinch. Cut-down Aberdeen blues with whipped or snelled snoods are a useful alternative.

These hooks have sharp points, fine bends and just enough temper in the wire to hold a heavy fish. You need the security of steel to hold a decent eel during the fight – they are surprisingly hard on hooks despite the small, soft mouth – but the wire must straighten in response to a quick, powerful jerk on the snood. The quickest

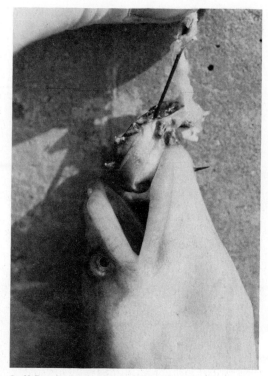

Pull firmly on the fine wire hook so that the bend springs open and snaps free.

A specimen eel of 2½lb taken from an estuary sea wall.

and safest way to unhook eels and flatties is to jerk the hook until the bend straightens. In matchfishing where every second counts, you cannot afford to bother with disgorgers.

Tactics

The right hook and trace guarantee plenty of eel bites. Tight lines and grip wired sinkers drive the hook into the eel's jaws rather than have it sucked into the back of the throat. Help matters along by striking

111

hard as soon as the bite develops. Eels usually rattle the tip a couple of times, then whack it down. That is when you grab the rod and hit them. Timing and secure hooking count heavily towards tangle-free fishing as well as putting more eels in the pan. If all goes according to plan most of your eels will be hooked neatly. Sound hooking is very important for prevention of tangles. As soon as you feel the fish on the line, crank and pump it ashore as quickly as you can. Give no more leeway than strictly necessary to avoid snap-offs. You need to have that eel moving fast as it breaks water. Never let it touch dry land: an eel that gets a grip will make knotted nylon of your trace in a flash.

Whistled through mid-air straight into your hand, an eel is so much easier to control. If you are really quick you can jerk out the hook and dump the fish in a bucket before it has time to orientate itself and start lashing. High-speed landing is the only way to avoid monumental snarl-ups. Newspaper, scouring pads and the other gadgets for handling a lively eel are unnecessary. One useful tip is to grab the sinker and pull the line tight against the rod tip so that the eel on its snood hangs clear of the main rig until you have time to grab it.

Baits

Eels are far from single-minded about baits. Ragworms, sand-eels, fish strips and even lugworms are fair targets for beach eels but in the long run it pays to concen-trate your efforts on crabs, peelers especially. Some fishermen reckon to use some 8,000 crabs in the average year's match and pleasure fishing. Along the way they pick up some useful tricks for presentation that boost results with eels, flatties and other species besides.

Fishermen who insist on the best usually collect their own crabs. Sound advice to anglers who must rely on commercial supplies is to shop around for fresh peelers rather than moth-eaten, barely alive creatures that have not seen the beach this last fortnight. Once you have found your crabs, look after them. Cool, wet weeds and darkness are the right formula for keeping peelers perky.

How-to-do-it articles on peeler fishing usually recommend shucking off the carapace, taking off the legs, chopping the crab into manageable chunks and threading it on to the hook, perhaps finally securing it with shearing elastic. It is a good way to lose bites because crabs prepared like this catch nowhere near as many eels. First you must get rid of every scrap of hard shell, even the bits underneath. Pull off the legs and peel back the top shell, then turn the crab upside down and flip back the 'tail' with your finger. Peel it clean.

Now work your way over the crab, picking off every last scrap of calcified shell from the 'shoulders', mouth, leg stumps and belly. Pull out the gills as well. The job is not finished until the crab looks and feels exactly like the tenderest and juiciest softie you ever saw. Small crab are hooked whole: but because all-round eel and flatty

(Opposite) Swing the eel straight into your hand so that it cannot wrap itself in the trace.

bashing works out to be more economical and just as effective with two-pence piece sized offerings, you can cut your peelers into at least two baits per crab. Knives are useless for chopping such soft meat, so use sharp scissors instead. Mounted properly, baits stick to the hook with no need for strands of thread or rubber bands. The easiest method involves nothing more than sewing the point of the hook three or four times through the meat and skin sandwich until point and bend are bedded securely inside.

12 Tope and pollack

Tope

Big tope hooked from the shore are fast and powerful, perhaps the most sporting of inshore species in European waters. Forty and fifty pound fish test tackle and angler to the limit. Conger excepted, they are the premier target for beach fishermen. Yet even in a full season of fishing only a handful of real specimens are taken on rod and line from beaches and rocks. Nobody has determined why tope are so reluctant to venture close inshore or why some regions that offer excellent offshore fishing are barren within two or three miles of the beach. The deep offshore channels of the outer Thames and Essex river estuaries are alive with them – small fish in plague proportions plus dozens of thirty to fifty pounders and a few over sixty pounds. Inshore it is a different tale: the closer to land you fish, the fewer tope are boated and the smaller they are. From the beach a tope of more than five pounds is a rarity.

Water depth may be involved but it is far from the whole explanation. Over on the Atlantic coast, in Cornwall, Wales and particularly in the far west of Ireland it is not at all uncommon to hook tope – big fish at that – from three to four feet of gin clear water lying over clean, flat sand. The better fishing is linked to overcast daylight or night but on occasions tope feed in bright sunshine as well, taking no notice of swimmers.

The essential difference between good marks for beach and rock tope, and the many areas of Britain which miss out, concerns food chains and natural cycles of the sea. Atlantic water with its rich crop of plankton, mackerel and sand-eels is closely involved. Mackerel and sand-eels figure high on the tope's diet, so theoretically one might conclude that wherever those bait fish migrate close inshore, tope fishing should be feasible. It does seem to work out that way.

Some years ago tope from the shore shared top honours with surf bassing as *the* way to fish. Mike Osborne and Stanley Hosking of Camborne, leading lights of the Cornish angling scene, landed dozens of specimen tope from the deep-water coves and headlands of Cornwall between Land's End and Trevose Head. The pair cut a notch in the gaff handle for every fish over forty pounds, until eventually the shaft snapped because most of the wood had been chopped away. Anglers in Wales also produced a long list of big fish. In contrast to the Cornish tope which were for the most part rock-caught, the Welsh fire showed a more even balance between rock and sandy beach.

Since then tope fishing has declined in the west to some extent. Whatever the ecological reasons may be, some blame at least falls on anglers who kill tope indiscriminately. By far the worst culprits were those fishing the tope festivals. Hundreds of quality tope were killed, brought ashore for weighing then kicked into the harbour.

*A favourite tope mark in the West of Ireland where fish are
virtually guaranteed in the right conditions.*

Organisers and fishermen involved in that
annual slaughter are directly responsible
for the redressed balance of tope fishing.

Today's best toping is offshore of the east
coast of England. Though decent pockets
of sport remain in the west and in Wales,
and as far north as Luce Bay, the western
tope stocks have fallen well short of their
past glory. Maybe they will come back;
there is no reason to think otherwise. On
the other hand, now mackerel have also
been slaughtered it is difficult for the
Atlantic coastline to support its former

number of predators. As a consequence,
shore tope fishing in the United Kingdom
is now much harder work than it used
to be.

Habits

Tope run in packs offshore, and in small
groups or alone closer to the shore. They
move with the tide, hunting where currents and headlands concentrate baitfish.
Deep water is sometimes a decisive factor.
Add them all together and you arrive at an

ideal tope mark – a rock ledge on a headland washed by strong tides. Some tope are constantly moving with the tide, so cast your tackle right into the stream. Others, like pike on a fast-moving river, take up station alongside the main current and wait for food to come to them in the gigantic eddy where the headland meets open sea. Unfortunately, pinpointing the best marks is difficult. There is no worthwhile alternative to local knowledge; if there is a subject that demands a great deal of homework, it is tope location.

Hotspots are localised in the extreme. Two hundred yards can make the difference between good tope fishing and wasted effort. I believe you stand little hope of consistent sport unless you live locally or have a contact who does know the area. Exact timing counts as well: spring and summer marks may be useless in autumn, and the lunar cycle is always critically important. It sounds a gloomy prospect for anglers who have never hooked a tope from the shore; there is no point in disguising that. But if you are an angler who lives in a good area or travels there often enough to justify the extra effort, you may as well cast a second rod rigged for tope. There is nothing to lose and you could just as easily latch on to a big ray, conger or even a giant bass.

I believe that the main area in Europe which offers a good chance of tope on a regular basis for non-specialist fishermen is Ireland, with the bottom end of Scotland coming in a close second if you fish the right weeks. I know that unless I go fishing with a local Cornish or Welsh angler, my chances of a shore tope are virtually nil. I rate them fifty–fifty in Scotland without local assistance. But I am 95 per cent certain I could find one or two fish during a week's fishing in south-west Eire during May to October.

Tackle and baits

It is fortunate that tope fishing is seldom the realm of the big caster. Baby tournament multiplier reels are completely out of step with heavy, fast-running tope which strip off 100 yards or more of line on the first run. Very big fish hooked in shallow, sandy-bottomed channels or from the edges of a surf beach rip off twice as much with ease. Less than 300 yards of line is a mistake. Breaking strain is nowhere near as important. Ordinary 12–18lb test monofilament will do nicely. Length of line, not strength, makes the difference with all long-running species; even 50lb line cannot hold a 25lb fish making its first run.

Were the gears faster and spools stronger, small multipliers could just about handle big tope. The trouble lies in the retrieve rate. Any small multiplier half-empty of line has a pitiful winding speed, and for tope as for bass and big cod come to that, you can never afford slack line. Sometimes the fish runs fast against the clutch then doubles back, generating fifty yards or more of loose line. Fishermen using tiny reels wind like mad and finally tighten up to discover that the fish has long since slipped the hook. A faster reel whips back line and reconnects you with the tope. Big reels like the ABU 900C and Penn Magpower 970/980 are far superior to 6500CT-type baitcasters.

Suitable tope baits range from a fillet of mackerel to a whole dab. Sand-eels should be at least six inches long, bigger if you can get them. While tope seldom insist on massive baits, you generally find it necessary to cast quite a chunk of sinker and terminal

Mike Millman

rig as well. Even though an 80 to 120 yard cast is far enough, the rod still needs a fair backbone to cope. Ordinary 5–6oz beach rods are fine. Fast action and a stiff butt are a little less useful than medium-fast action which offers smoother casting of heavy, bulky end tackle and baits. Ultra-rapid rods are a serious liability on a rock ledge where space is too tight for a big pendulum-style swing.

Start the trace with a strong 40–50lb shock leader. Make it longer than normal so that if necessary you can handline the fish as it comes to gaff. Gaffing is not necessary from the surf, but the extra length of leader is still valuable for controlling a tope that thrashes in the backwash. Thread on a small but strong link swivel or swivel/split ring. Now tie a second swivel or split ring to the end of the heavy nylon. The trace is connected to this lower swivel, producing a neat running leger rig.

A very sharp O'Shaughnessy or Model Perfect 4/0–6/0 is better than the traditional meat hook. Smaller hooks are sharper, penetrate better and are more than strong enough; 6/0s are about the limit for long-range penetration. Switch to ultra-tough Seamasters if you like, but they really must be quite small. Tremendously thick wire and long point are almost impossible to sink below barb level on size 2/0 and over.

Six to twelve inches of 100lb stainless wire crimped between hook eye and lower swivel is adequate to ward off sharp teeth. The tope's rough skin is handled by the

strong leader, which is far more pliable and easier to cast than wire. A 5–6oz sinker, plain for slow water, grip wired for fast tides, produces good distances with big baits and is light enough not to hamper the tope from moving away with the trace. Tope are not especially fussy about bait presentation but you may as well stack the odds in your favour.

Tactics

Tope arrive inshore at any stage of tide depending on location and season. A rising tide and the first hours of the ebb are universally popular with tope anglers; it helps if tides are making up towards springs. An evening high tide is useful as well, the best sport being around mid-afternoon until just after dark. Night fishing and early dawn favours shallow surf beaches where tope are reluctant feeders in daylight. Again, that is a generalisation: many a big tope has arrived at midday when not an inch of swell disturbed the shoreline.

Tope fishing is a wait-and-see game of long periods of inactivity intercut with spells of rapid bites. It is a fair bet that if you do hook a tope, another is lurking out there ready for your next bait to hit the water. Two or three fishermen often hook fish at the same time, which is good reason to use one rod each and not to cram too many anglers on the same patch. Life is hectic enough without knitting together half a dozen lines.

Tope bites vary considerably. Some fish

(Opposite) Successful tope fishing demands strict attention to detail and much hard work. Even then, there is an element of luck.

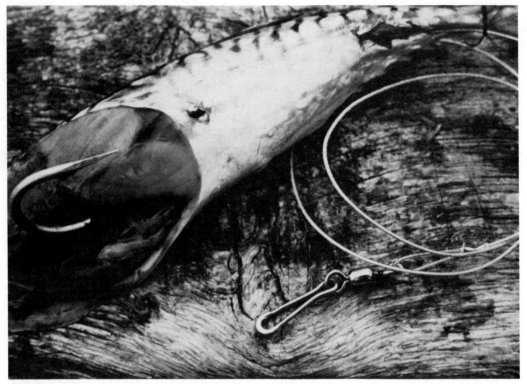

Half a fresh mackerel on a strong hook attached to a short piece of 100lb wire.

creep away so slowly you notice nothing until you start to wind in. Others hit so hard and run so fast you have to pounce on the rod before it disappears. Most tope pick up the bait – well signalled on the rod tip – and move away quite gently until you strike. Then they tear off at high speed. If the clutch is not present, say goodbye to fish, terminal rig and 100 yards of line.

Eventually it will stop, and then you can pump line back on to the spool. On clean ground the rest of the fight is divided into a series of weakening runs and line recovery. A good tope fights itself right out. When it does drift into tailing or gaff range it is exhausted and easily lifted out. Fresh fish bullied quickly inshore on heavy tackle are a handful. Watch out for the trace and hook rather than the teeth. Bites are much rarer than hands severely cut by a whirling trace. Never lift a fish by the wire. Aim for its tail instead.

Pollack

Pollack and cod are species of the same family. While cod are essentially bottom dwellers, pollack roam between surface and sea-bed most commonly in deep water with plenty of inshore cover. Big pollack prefer to remain offshore, hunting on reefs and wrecks which support pouting, sand-eels and other small bait fish. Inshore fish are generally much smaller, averaging less than 5lb on most rock marks. Only exceptionally are 10–12lb pollack landed from the rocks. Like a 10lb bass, a double figure pollack is something of a prize in beach fishing circles and often eludes the keenest of anglers. No doubt more would be caught

if pollack fishing basked in the same glory as bassing. But it remains a minority sport even among anglers who spend much of their time fishing over the right ground.

Casting from an open beach with normal bottom tackle, you might pick up plenty of small/medium pollack if the shoreline is weedy and full of rocks. Exceptionally, wide-open surf strands attract pollack into extreme casting range. Sand-eels cast for smalleyed rays and bass are snatched by fish hunting the flat sand.

Pollack are far easier to locate and hook

Tope sometimes move into the surf onwards of late evening. Calmer water may bring them right up to the edge.

from rock marks. Deep inshore water, dense cover and plenty of baitfish are the key – the environment is perfect for a species of fish that lies in wait for its food. Pollack certainly do scavenge but unlike cod, which feed that way most of the time, they show a distinct preference for a moving, lively bait a few feet off the bottom. Floatfishing and spinning are the best option for shore pollack. Spinning is more fun and attracts a cross-section of fish. Big pollack, where they venture into casting range, are less responsive to artificials. A filleted half-mackerel or six inch sand-eel legered on clean sand near rocky outcrops might hit the jackpot but is still more likely to lure a ray, conger or big bass – not that anyone would object.

Spinning tactics

Light spinning tackle and 10lb line are strong enough for general pollack spinning. In dense cover you might step up to 15lb tackle regardless of the fish's weight. Pollack dive hard immediately they feel the hook. You must hold them back or lose your terminal rig. Short spinning rods are fine for casting and working the lure. An eight foot rod fits the bill pretty well but an extra two feet on the tip is sometimes beneficial for guiding hooked fish around inshore rock ledges and kelp beds. Sinkers and lures under an ounce cast better on a fixed spool reel. Two ounces is the minimum weight which produces easy casting and controllable line flow on multipliers. Choose which reel you personally prefer.

What you gain in smoothness and drag versatility on a multiplier is lost in retrieve speed. A well-made fixed spool is adequately braked and has the advantage of rapid winding.

Metal spoons and spinners are excellent but expensive pollack lures. Silver, gold and red blades two to three inches long are heavy enough to cast 75 yards or more from the rocks, they sink quickly in even moderate swells and work smoothly at chosen depth. Light spinners tend to rise to the surface as you wind them in, often planing high over the fish's heads. Pollack normally cruise in the lower half of the water and although they will come up a few feet to grab a bait they seldom waste their strength chasing food near the surface. Like many fish that live on rocks and reefs they are strongly territorial.

Lure design is seldom critical. Toby spoons and German sprats are traditionally successful. Colour does make a difference: the pollack's taste changes overnight. Red one day, silver the next – you cannot be sure unless you experiment. Strange as it may seem, black is highly successful in low light or even at night. If all else fails add a mackerel strip to the spinner. Baited spoons trigger bites when movement alone fails to arouse. Pollack will even take a baited spoon allowed to fall to the bottom. Redgill sand-eels spun slowly close to rocks and weeds are extremely good. They are too light to cast alone, so attach an eel about three feet behind a small bomb or drilled bullet sinker. You need at least two feet of trace to

(Opposite) Pollack mark on the open coast, with deep water and plenty of underwater cover.

prevent the sinker killing the lure's action. Fish Redgills slowly for best results.

Artificial baits are expensive. The occasional loss is acceptable and inevitable but few anglers are prepared to throw away a dozen a day. Slow-moving baits like Redgills fished close to the rough ground produce plenty of pollack but cost a fortune. There is no alternative to casting the bait close to the rocks, so the answer has to be another lure. Try a real sand-eel, live or frozen. In the long run sand-eels are the best bait anyway, fished on the bottom, floated or spun. The snag is finding them when you want to go fishing. Pollack experts consider it worth going to the trouble of raking, netting or even buying the real thing. You catch more fish, and the cost of losing baits is so small that you do not mind casting a sand-eel into dirty ground which would be suicidal to tackle with lures.

Random casting seldom locates pollack from the rocks. The whole of the water should be covered with the bait before you move on to another spot. Cast in a fan-like pattern and search the water from bottom to top as well. First cast, throw the lure straight out as far as you can. Leave the reel out of gear so that line flows into the sea until the lure hits the sea-bed. From the moment it splashes into the sea until it ceases to fall, count off the seconds in your head.

Suppose it takes twenty seconds to hit bottom: slip the reel back into gear, lift the rod tip to raise the tackle a few inches then retrieve slowly. Feel the trace work its way

inshore and be ready for bites and snags. The lure will probably snag bottom at least once on the way in. On extremely rough ground you could lose the lot. It does not matter now you know the lie of the land.

Cast the same distance and direction again but leave the tackle to sink for fifteen seconds before starting to retrieve. The lost five seconds are enough to hold the tackle a couple of feet above the sea-bed; high enough to miss the rocks and weeds, still low enough to attract pollack. If the sea-bed is evenly sloped without rock piles and high-standing snags, you can now move on to cover the whole area by placing a series of casts in a fan-like pattern across the mark. Expect to hook a fish any time. Pollack sometimes lie right under your feet.

Now work the next higher layer of water: sink the tackle for, say, ten seconds before starting to retrieve. This time be very careful about the last twenty yards as the lure swims across open water before nearing the rocks. Pollack will hit at the last minute then dive straight down. Sometimes it pays to work downwards from the surface but as a rule pollack stay deep, so it saves time if you begin at the sea-bed and work up.

A pollack bite is distinctive. You may feel a preliminary tug, but the main attack is a savage pull on the rod tip which stops the lure dead. Then the fish dives – and nothing dives like a scared pollack. Presetting the clutch saves line from immediate danger but does not prevent snagging of course. Here you take pot luck. If you

(Opposite) Average inshore pollack are under five pounds, with only the rare specimen in double figures.

hold the fish against a tight line you might snap off. If the pollack reaches the sea-bed he will sneak into the densest cover available.

The best bet is to give a preliminary couple of feet of line against the drag, then thumb the spool hard while you raise the rod tip high. Lift the fish, turn him away from the dive-path and chances are he will fight it out near the surface. Pollack are not particularly stubborn after that first run and they do not qualify for the list of hardest fighting species. If the line survives the first thirty seconds, life will be smooth and uneventful. Use a landing net to lift the beaten fish. Gaffs are totally inappropriate for this species which a majority of anglers prefer to return.

(Opposite) Small fish invade harbours in summer. Spinning and float fishing are the easy methods of hooking them.

127

Other fishing books published by The Crowood Press

Travels with a Two Piece *John Bailey*
A collection of writing inspired by the author's journeys along the rivers of England
with an ancient two piece fly fishing rod.

River Fishing *Len Head*
How to read waters and set about catching the major coarse fishing species.

Boat Fishing *Mike Millman, Richard Stapley and John Holden*
A concise but detailed guide to modern boat fishing.

Stillwater Coarse Fishing *Melvyn Russ*
A guide to the maze of tackle, baits, tactics and techniques that surround the cream
of coarse fishing in Britain.

My Way with Trout *Arthur Cove*
Outlines the techniques and tactics employed by the master of nymph fishing on
stillwaters.

In Visible Waters *John Bailey*
John Bailey reveals the deep insight that he has gained over nearly thirty years
closely observing the lives of the coarse fishing species.

Imitations of the Trout's World *Bob Church and Peter Gathercole*
Describes advanced fly tying techniques and explores the link between the natural
and the artificial.

Fly Fishing for Salmon and Sea Trout *Arthur Oglesby*
The first recent really comprehensive work to deal almost exclusively with fly
fishing techniques.

Tench *Len Head*
Natural history, physiology, distribution, tackle tactics and techniques are
discussed in this most comprehensive study of the species.

Pike – The Predator becomes the Prey *John Bailey and Martyn Page*
Twenty top pike anglers, experience of all types of waters.

Carp – The Quest for the Queen *John Bailey and Martyn Page*
Combined specialist knowledge from twenty-six big fish men.

Long Distance Casting *John Holden*
A guide to tackle and techniques of long-range casting in saltwater.

The Beach Fisherman's Tackle Guide *John Holden*
Covers, rods, reels, accessories, rigs and maintenance.

An Introduction to Reservoir Trout Fishing *Alan Pearson*
Covers tackle, casting, flies, bank and boat fishing, and location.

Rods and Rod Building *Len Head*
A manual of rod building, giving guidance on design and the selection of rods.

Further information from **The Crowood Press (0672) 20320**